T0254882

Lecture Notes in Computer Science 13187

Ayoub Nouri · Weimin Wu · Kamel Barkaoui ·
ZhiWu Li (Eds.)

Verification and Evaluation of Computer and Communication Systems

15th International Conference, VECoS 2021
Virtual Event, November 22–23, 2021
Revised Selected Papers

Springer

Editors
Ayoub Nouri
Huawei Grenoble Research Center
Grenoble, France

Weimin Wu
Zhejiang University
Hangzhou, China

Kamel Barkaoui
CNAM-CEDRIC
Paris Cedex 03, France

ZhiWu Li
Macau University of Science and Technology
Macau, Macao

ISSN 0302-9743 ISSN 1611-3349 (electronic)
Lecture Notes in Computer Science
ISBN 978-3-030-98849-4 ISBN 978-3-030-98850-0 (eBook)
https://doi.org/10.1007/978-3-030-98850-0

This Springer imprint is published by the registered company Springer Nature Switzerland AG
The registered company address is: Gewerbestrasse 11, 6330 Cham, Switzerland

Preface

This volume contains the papers presented at the 15th International Conference on Verification and Evaluation of Computer and Communication Systems (VECoS 2021), held as a virtual conference during November 22-23, 2021 due to the COVID-19 pandemic. The conference was planned to take place in Beijing, China.

This year's event continues the tradition of previous editions 2007 in Algiers Algeria, 2008 in Leeds UK, 2009 in Rabat Morocco, 2010 in Paris France, 2011 in Tunis Tunisia, 2012 in Paris France, 2013 in Florence Italy, 2014 in Béjaïa Algeria, 2015 in Bucharest Romania, 2016 in Tunis Tunisia, 2017 in Montreal Canada, 2018 in Grenoble France, 2019 in Porto Portugal, and 2020 in Xi'an China (virtual).

As in previous editions, VECoS 2021 provided a forum for researchers and practitioners in the areas of verification, control, performance, and dependability evaluation in order to discuss the state of the art and challenges in modern computer and communication systems in which functional and extra-functional properties are strongly interrelated. The main motivation is to encourage cross-fertilization between various formal verification and evaluation approaches, methods, and techniques, and especially those developed for concurrent and distributed hardware/software systems.

The following events were co-located with the VECoS 2021 conference

- 24th International Symposium on Formal Methods
- 7th Symposium on Dependable Software Engineering
- 19th ACM-IEEE International Conference on Formal Methods and Models for System Design

The Program Committee of VECoS 2021 was composed of 52 researchers from 18 countries. We received 12 full submissions from 11 countries. After a thorough and lively discussion phase, the committee decided to accept 5 papers including 4 regular and 1 position paper. Presented topics spanned over different subjects, namely approaches to enhance formal verification scalability end efficiency, contract-based techniques for safety-critical timed systems, and verification of multi-agent systems. The conference also included two invited talks on distributed systems monitoring and intelligent data-driven systems. An invited paper for the former is included in this volume.

We are grateful to the Program and Organizing Committee members, to the reviewers for their cooperation, and to Springer for their professional support during the production phase of the proceedings. We are also thankful to all authors of submitted papers, the invited speakers, and to all participants of the conference. Their interest in this conference and contributions are greatly appreciated.

November 2021

Ayoub Nouri
Weimin Wu

Organization

VECoS 2021 was planned to take place in Beijing, China, November 22-23, 2021. Due to the COVID-19 pandemic, VECoS 2021 was held as a virtual conference.

Executive Committee

Program Co-chairs

Ayoub Nouri	Huawei, France
Weimin Wu	Zhejiang University, China

General Co-chairs

Kamel Barkaoui	CEDRIC-Cnam, France
Zhiwu Li	Macau University of Science and Technology, China

Publicity Co-chairs

Belgacem Ben Hedia	CEA-List, France
Gaiyun Liu	Xidian University, China
Vladimir-Alexandru Paun	Five Rescue, France

Steering Committee

Djamil Aissani	LaMOS, Université de Bejaia, Algeria
Mohamed Faouzi Atig	Uppsala University, Sweden
Kamel Barkaoui (Chair)	CEDRIC-Cnam, France
Hanifa Boucheneb	VeriForm, Polytechnique Montreal, Canada
Francesco Flammini	Ansaldo STS, Italy
Belgacem Ben Hedia	CEA-List Saclay, France
Mohamed Kaâniche	LAAS-CNRS, France
Bruno Monsuez	U2IS, ENSTA Paris, France
Nihal Pekergin	LACL Université Paris-Est Créteil, France
Tayssir Touili	LIPN, CNRS, Université Paris Nord, France

Referees

Yasmina Abdeddaim	Université Gustave Eiffel, France
Djamil Aissani	LaMOS, Université de Bejaia, Algeria
Yamine A. Ameur	IRIT, INPT-ENSEEIHT, France
Mihail Asavoae	CEA-List, France
Mohamed Faouzi Atig	Uppsala University, Sweden
Eric Badouel	Inria, France
Kamel Barkaoui	CEDRIC-Cnam, France
Belgacem Ben Hedia	CEA-List, France
Adel Benzina	Tunisia Polytechnic School, Tunisia
Patrice Bonhomme	Université de Tours, France
Hanifa Boucheneb	VeriForm, Polytechnique Montreal, Canada
Yu-Fang Chen	Academia Sinica, Taiwan
Zhenbang Chen	National University of Defense Technology, China
Feng Chu	Université d'Evry Val d'Essonne, France
Gabriel Ciobanu	Romanian Institute of Computer Science, Romania
Jean-Michel Couvreur	Université d'Orléans, France
Isabel Demongodin	Université Aix-Marseille, France
Annie Geniet	Université de Poitiers, France
Mohamed Ghazel	Université Gustave Eiffel, France
Serge Haddad	ENS Cachan, France
Peter Hofner	Australian National University, Australia
Akram Idani	Université Grenoble Alpes, France
Mohamed Jmaiel	University of Sfax, Tunisia
Jorge Julvez	University of Cambridge, UK
Kais Klai	Université Paris 13, France
Moez Krichen	Al-Baha University, Saudi Arabia
Sébastien Lahaye	Polytech Angers, France
Axel Legay	Université Catholique de Louvain, Belgium
Ondrej Lengal	Brno University of Technology, Czech Republic
Alexei Lisitsa	University of Liverpool, UK
Gaiyun Liu	Xidian University, China
Eric Madelaine	Inria, France
Roland Meyer	TU Braunschweig, Germany
Ali Mili	New Jersey Institute of Technology, USA
Bruno Monsuez	U2IS, ENSTA Paris, France
Mohamed Mosbah	INP Bordeaux, France
Ayoub Nouri	Huawei France, France
Catuscia Palamidessi	École Polytechnique Palaiseau, France
Vladimir-Alexandru Paun	Five Rescue, France

Geguang Pu	East China Normal University, China
Shengchao Qin	Teesside University, UK
Ameur-Boulifa Rabéa	Telecom Paris, France
Sirdey Renaud	CEA, France
Riadh Robbana	University of Carthage, Tunisia
Ricardo J. Rodriguez	Universidad de Zaragoza, Spain
Arnaud Sangnier	Université Paris 7, France
Layth Sliman	Efrei Paris, France
Tayssir Touili	LIPN, CNRS, Université Paris Nord, France
Katinka Wolter	Freie Universitaet zu Berlin, Germany
Weimin Wu	Zhejiang University Hangzhou, China

Additional Reviewers

Nourelhouda Souid	Université Paris 13, France
Sarbojit Das	Uppsala University, Sweden
Peter Riviere	IRIT, France
Cheng Wen	Teesside University, UK
Yi Li	Chongqing Institutes of Green and Intelligent Technology, China
Zhiwu Xu	Shenzhen University, China

Sponsoring Institutions

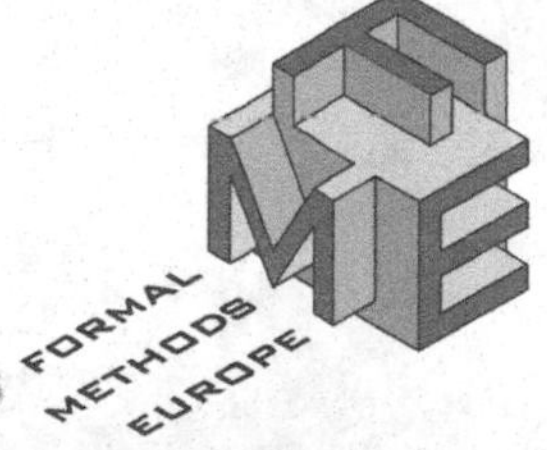

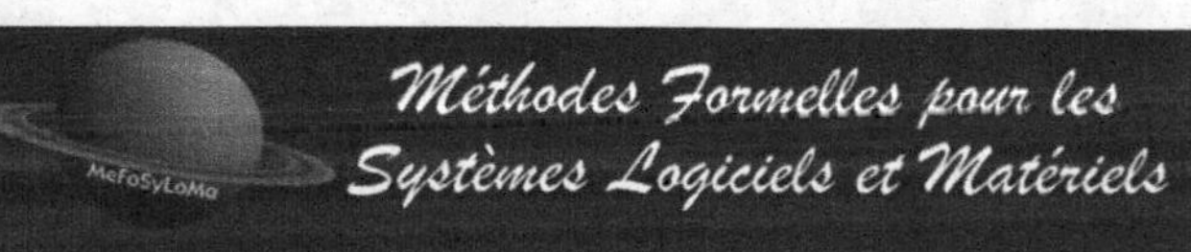

Contents

On Decentralized Monitoring

Yliès Falcone(✉)

Univ. Grenoble Alpes, CNRS, Inria, Grenoble INP, LIG, 38000 Grenoble, France
ylies.falcone@univ-grenoble-alpes.fr

Abstract. This paper overviews some approaches to decentralized monitoring, where one considers systems with units of computation that are physically or logically distributed. Such systems are checked against specifications referring to the global behavior of the system. The problems that arise are (i) the absence of global observation point in the system, (ii) the partial view and evaluation of specifications on each component, and (iii) the need for communication. Decentralized monitoring addresses the placement of runtime monitors and their communication strategies, as well as the techniques, algorithms, and tools to make monitoring effective in such context.

1 Introduction

Runtime Verification. Runtime verification [3,27,28] (aka monitoring) refers to the collection of techniques for observing and analyzing the behavior of systems during their execution against some desired properties. Runtime Verification is a lightweight but incomplete technique that can be complementary to other verification techniques. In runtime verification, one uses a so-called *monitor* that serves as a decision procedure for each of the properties being monitored.

Motivations for Decentralizing the Monitoring Process. On the one hand, since processor frequency has stabilized over the past years [9], more systems are being designed to be decentralized to benefit from multiple computation units (cores or processors). Examples of decentralized systems with independent computation units abound (e.g., modern cars, decentralized finance systems, robot swarms [42], collaborative tasks using Unmanned Aerial Vehicles (UAVs) or micro-UAVs [12]). On the other hand, the users wanting to monitor such systems often perceive them as monolithic systems which, seen from the outside, exhibit a uniform behavior as opposed to many components displaying many local behaviors that together constitute the system's global

This paper is based on previous publications [5,7,10,11,17,18,21,24] of the author with colleagues. I thank Jean-Claude Fernandez, Ayoub Nouri, and Victor Roussalany for their comments on an early version of this paper. I would like to gratefully acknowledge the support from the H2020-ECSEL-2018-IA call - Grant Agreement number 826276 (CPS4EU), the European Union's Horizon 2020 research and innovation programme - Grant Agreement number 956123 (FOCETA), from the French ANR project ANR-20-CE39-0009 (SEVERITAS), the Auvergne-Rhône-Alpes research project MOAP, and LabEx PERSYVAL-Lab (ANR-11-LABX-0025-01) funded by the French program Investissement d'avenir.

A. Nouri et al. (Eds.): VECoS 2021, LNCS 13187, pp. 1–16, 2022.
https://doi.org/10.1007/978-3-030-98850-0_1

behavior. This level of abstraction is often reasonable, hiding implementation details from users who may want to specify the system's global behavior.

In decentralized systems, it is desirable to decentralize the monitoring process for several reasons, such as reducing the number and size of required messages as well as the computation needed to reach a verdict, and balancing the required computation.

The problem addressed by decentralized runtime verification is then how such specifications can actually be monitored in a distributed system that has no central data collection point, with the above objectives in mind.

Assumptions. We emphasize the assumptions in our work on decentralized runtime verification. First, we assume that the local behavior of all components is (sufficiently) observable. Then, we assume the existence of a *global clock* in the system of which the local monitors are aware. This assumption is realistic for several critical industrial systems (e.g., [35,43,49]), including those where the system at hand is composed of several applications executing on the same operating system, or where a synchronous bus (e.g., FlexRay) provides the global clock. Furthermore, we direct the reader to [2] for a real application of our work [7] on networked embedded systems. Second, we assume that the monitors can communicate directly with each other in a reliable fashion: any message sent is supposed to eventually arrive unaltered to its destination.[1] However, in the most general form of our work, we do Introduction make any assumptions on the preservation of the order of messages sent by each monitor.

We note that the presented approaches are not yet ready to handle distributed systems in their full generality as two of their important features are not supported, namely the absence of a global clock and the possibility of loosing messages. However, we directly target the problem of physically separating the computation done by monitors observing partial information on the system global behavior. Thus, the presented work can be seen as a step towards achieving distributed runtime verification of distributed systems.

Problem Statement. In the decentralized setting, the system is composed of several (black box) components $C_1, \ldots, C_n$ for some $n \in \mathbb{N} \setminus \{0\}$ ($\mathbb{N}$ being the set of natural numbers) running on the same clock where each component C_i has a local set of atomic propositions of interest AP_i. A local monitor can be attached to each component so that with instrumentation each component can produce a local trace of events, which at time $t \in \mathbb{N}$ is $u_i(0) \cdots u_i(t)$ where $u_i(t') \in 2^{AP_i}$ is the event emitted at time $t' \leq t$. Furthermore, the specification of the system is given by a formal property φ defined over $\cup_{i\in[1,n]} AP_i$. Property φ denotes a set of traces $\mathcal{L}(\varphi)$, which is a subset of Σ^* or Σ^ω depending on the specification formalism used to describe φ. Note that in general $2^{\cup_{i\in[1,n]} AP_i} \neq \cup_{i\in[1,n]} 2^{AP_i}$, implying in particular that the evaluation of the specification (i) cannot be performed on components in isolation, and (ii) imposes communication.

The decentralized monitoring problem then consists in checking the (virtual) global trace of the system (that can be reconstructed from the local traces) $\mathbf{u} = u_1(0) \cup \ldots \cup u_n(0) \cdot u_1(1) \cup \ldots \cup u_n(1) \cdots u_1(t) \cup \ldots \cup u_n(t)$ against φ at any time $t' \leq t$.

[1] Algorithms can be used for guaranteeing the absence of message loss in distributed systems, see [40] for instance.

A decentralized monitoring algorithm is expected to have the following properties: it should be sound and complete. Soundness means that if the decentralized monitoring algorithm reports a verdict (true denoted by $\top$ or false denoted by $\bot$), then such a verdict corresponds to the evaluation of the global trace on the monitored specification. Completeness means that if the global trace evaluates to $\top$ or $\bot$, then the decentralized monitoring algorithm eventually reports such verdict.

Several communication protocols may be used by local monitors to communicate and reach a global verdict. For instance, communication can be considered as instantaneous and the monitors are allowed to send an arbitrary number of messages to each other between two system steps[2], as is the case in [10]. Communication can be considered as having a fixed latency depending on the global clock. For instance, [7] assumes that the communication between monitors occurs between ticks of the global clock and that any message sent at time t is received at time $t+1$. Another possibility is to design a decentralized monitoring algorithm and protocol so that no assumption is made wrt. the latency of messages, as in [24].

2 Considering Synchronous Communications and Linear-Temporal Logic Formulae [5,7]

Context and Motivations. Let φ be a Linear Temporal Logic (LTL, cf. [41,47]) formula formalizing a property over the system's global behavior. We aim to design a decentralized monitoring algorithm so that, every local monitor, M_i, will at any time, t, monitor its own LTL formula w.r.t. a partial behavioral trace, u_i. Let us use $u_i(m)$ to denote the $(m+1)$-th event in a trace u_i, and $\mathbf{u} = (u_1, u_2, \ldots, u_n)$ for the *global trace*, obtained by pair-wise parallel composition of the partial traces, each of which at time t is of length $t+1$ (i.e., $\mathbf{u} = u_1(0) \cup \ldots \cup u_n(0) \cdot u_1(1) \cup \ldots \cup u_n(1) \cdots u_1(t) \cup \ldots \cup u_n(t)$, a sequence of union sets). We shall refer to partial traces as local traces due to their locality to a particular monitor in the system.

Contributions. In this line of work, we describe the decentralization of the classical progression function so that we obtain a decentralized monitoring algorithm as described above. We state the properties of our decentralized monitoring algorithm. This work was implemented in DecentMon, a tool described in Sect. 7.1.

Decentralized Progression. The decentralized monitoring algorithm is based on formula rewriting (also known as progression or derivation) which has been used for centralized monitoring, as seen for instance in [1,50]. Progression is based on the expansion laws of LTL and its fix-point semantics. In the decentralized setting, when some atomic proposition p is not part of an observation $\sigma \subseteq APi$ (i.e., $p \notin \sigma$) made on local component C_i, we need to distinguish between two reasons: the atomic proposition is not observable locally versus the atomic proposition does not hold on C_i. Then, we progress accordingly, adapting the progression rule for atomic propositions by parametrizing it

[2] We abstract away from clock and communication cycles and take a "step" to represent moments at which a fresh set of events becomes available to the monitor.

with a local set of atomic propositions APi. Whenever some atomic proposition p is progressed and $p \notin \sigma \wedge p \in APi$, atomic proposition p is progressed into $\overline{\mathbf{X}}p$ where $\overline{\mathbf{X}}$ means "previously" as in past-time LTL (cf. [39]). The intuition is that we register at the timestamp of progression that, at the next time stamp, p needs to hold at the previous timestamp.

Decentralized Monitoring Algorithm by Decentralized Progression. The decentralized monitoring algorithm evaluates the global trace $\mathbf{u}$ by considering the locally observed traces u_i, $i \in [1, n]$ in separation, and the local formula φ_i^t at any time t. However, in order to allow for the local detection of global violations (and satisfactions), monitors must be able to communicate, since their traces are only partial w.r.t. the global behavior of the system. The algorithm maintains formula φ_i^t that evolves using progression applied to the local observations and the messages received from the other monitors. Each monitor sends a message to the other monitor if its obligation contains an LTL formula that cannot be evaluated locally.

Properties of the Monitoring Algorithm. The monitoring algorithm enjoys the soundness and completeness properties.

- soundness If a local monitor yields by rewriting $\varphi_i^t = \bot$ (resp. $\varphi_i^t = \top$) on some component C_i by observing u_i, it implies that $\mathbf{u}\Sigma^\omega \subseteq \Sigma^\omega \setminus \mathcal{L}(\varphi)$ (resp. $\mathbf{u}\Sigma^\omega \subseteq \mathcal{L}(\varphi)$) holds where $\mathcal{L}(\varphi)$ is the set of infinite sequences in Σ^ω described by φ. That is, a locally observed violation (resp. satisfaction) is, in fact, a global violation (resp. satisfaction). Or, in other words, $\mathbf{u}$ is a bad (resp. good) prefix for φ.
- completeness If centralized monitoring by progression would detect that $\mathbf{u}\Sigma^\omega \subseteq \Sigma^\omega \setminus \mathcal{L}(\varphi)$ (resp. $\mathbf{u}\Sigma^\omega \subseteq \mathcal{L}(\varphi)$), one of the local monitors on some component C_i yields $\varphi_i^{t'} = \bot$ (resp. $\varphi_i^{t'} = \top$), $t' \geq t$, for an observation u_i', an extension of u_i, the local observation of $\mathbf{u}$ on C_i, because of some latency induced by decentralized monitoring.

Because of the time taken by monitors to communicate obligations to each other, there is a worst case *communication delay* between the occurrence and the detection of a good (resp. bad) trace by a good (resp. bad) prefix. The worst case occurs when an obligation needs to be processed by all monitors in the system. Hence, the delay depends on the number of monitors in the system, and is also the upper bound for the number of past events each monitor needs to store locally to be able to progress all occurring past obligations.

3 Organizing the Monitors [10,11]

Context and Motivations. In this work, we aim study the influence of the organization of decentralized monitors to propose dedicated monitoring algorithm for each organization. The two approaches presented in the preceding sections considered two organizations of the monitors: in a round-robin fashion where monitors follow some (circular) order and a dynamic organization where monitors communicate with the monitor that could better process the message/state of formula. Having algorithms for different organizations of monitors allow to adapt to the topology of the monitored system/machine/network.

Contributions. According to the computation performed by local monitors and their communication protocol, we categorize a decentralized monitoring solution under the setting of either orchestration, migration, or choreography (using terminology from [32]), using LTL as a reference instantiation:

Orchestration (see Fig. 1): Orchestration is the setting where a single monitor (either one of the monitors attached to local components or an additional monitor introduced in the system) carries out all the monitoring processing while receiving local events from the other local monitors. Orchestration forces most of the computation payload to be placed on the local monitor receiving the events, while reducing the computation of other monitors to sending their local events.

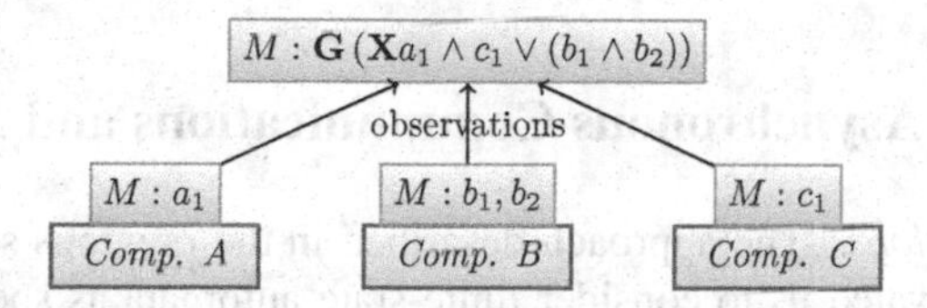

Fig. 1. An example of orchestration architecture.

Migration (see Fig. 2): Migration is the setting where the monitoring entity transports itself across the network, evolving as it goes along and following a predefined protocol (e.g., round robin)—abstracting away the need to transfer lower level (finer-grained) information.

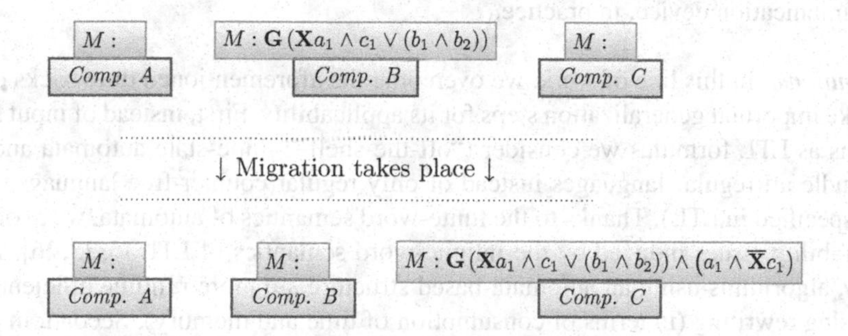

Fig. 2. An example of migration architecture

Choreography (see Fig. 3): Choreography is the setting where monitors are organized into a network and a protocol is used to enable cooperation between monitors. The synthesis of the communication network uses the structure of the monitored formula to place specialized monitors in charge of monitoring only a "projection" of the formula. Hence, compared to migration, choreography leverages the syntactic structure of the monitored formula and uses static information gathered from an offline analysis of the formula.

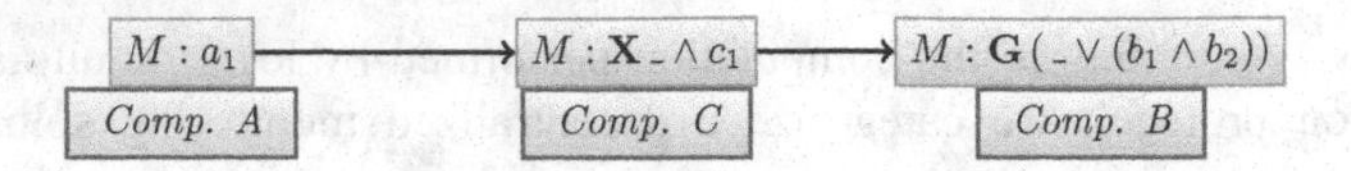

Fig. 3. An example of choreography architecture.

The three algorithms were implemented and integrated in the DecentMon tool. In our experiments, we compared the three approaches against the usual decentralized monitoring metrics. It allowed us to identify the behavior pattern of the algorithms using some randomly generated formulae and which algorithm performs better for each class of properties. For instance, orchestration shows best information delay, migration least number of messages, while choreography shows the smallest messages.

4 Considering Asynchronous Communications and Automata [24]

Context and Motivations. The approach described in the previous section suffer from limitations that motivated us to consider finite-state automata as specification formalism. First, it is assumed in [5,7] i) that at each time instant, monitors receive an event from the system and can communicate with each others, and ii) that communication does not take time. Second, the approach used LTL formulas to represent the local state of the monitor and progression (i.e., formula rewriting) each time a new event is received. A downside of progression, is the continuous growth of the size of local obligations with the length of trace; thus imposing a heavy overhead after 100 events. Finally, while [5,7] minimizes communication in terms of number of messages (i.e., obligations), it neglects their (continuously growing) size, with the risk of oversizing the communication device, in practice.

Contributions. In this line of work, we overcome the aforementioned drawbacks of [7] and make important generalization steps for its applicability. First, instead of input specifications as LTL formulas we consider ("off-the-shelf") finite-state automata and can thus handle all regular languages instead of only regular counter-free languages (that can be specified in LTL). Thanks to the finite-word semantics of automata, we avoid the monitorability issues induced by the infinite-word semantics of LTL [6,25,26]. Interestingly, algorithms using an automata-based structure are more runtime efficient than those using rewriting (in terms of consumption of time and memory). Second, in practice, communication and reception of events might not occur at the same rate or the communication device might become unavailable during monitoring; and such situations are handled by our algorithms.

Decentralization of a Monitor. Our decentralized monitors "estimate" the global state that would be obtained by a centralized monitor observing the events produced on all components. The estimation of the global state in the set of global states Q is modeled by a set of possible states (of the centralized monitor) given the (local) information received so far. The construction of the decentralized monitor resembles the power-set construction for finite-state automata but additionally account for partial information.

When a decentralized monitor receives an event (s, σ), it means that it is informed that the union of the atomic propositions that occurred on the components indexed in the set s is σ. The transition function is s.t. if the estimated global state is $\mathcal{Q} \in 2^Q \setminus \{\emptyset\}$ and it receives (s, σ) as event, then the estimated global state changes to $\Delta_\delta(\mathcal{Q}, s, \sigma)$ which contains all states s.t. one can find a transition in δ from a state in $\mathcal{Q}$ labeled with a global event σ' compatible with σ. Note that the size of Δ_δ is exponential in the size of δ, but Δ_δ is computed statically before monitoring. In other words, if the actual global state belongs to $\mathcal{Q}$, and the union of events that happen on components indexed in s is σ, then the actual global state belongs to $\Delta_\delta(\mathcal{Q}, s, \sigma)$ which is the set of states that can be reached from a state in $\mathcal{Q}$ with all possible global events (obtained by any observation that could happen on components indexed in $[1; n] \setminus s$). Regarding verdicts, a decentralized monitor emits the same verdict as a centralized one when the current state contains states of the centralized monitor that evaluate on the same verdict.

Decentralized Monitoring Algorithm. At an abstract level, the algorithm is an execution engine using a decentralized monitor. It computes the locally estimated global state of the system by aggregating information from events read locally and partial traces received from other monitors. It stores in q the last known global state of the system at time t_{last}, and in t the time instant of the last event received from the system.

Properties of Decentralized Monitoring. The algorithm enjoys similar properties as the one for monitoring LTL formulae, as described in the previous section, namely soundness and completeness (with delay), this time using the states of the underlying automaton. Since we consider asynchronous communications, the delay between the centralized and the decentralized cases can not be bounded.

5 Generalizing – Analytical Framework [21]

Execution History Encoding. An execution of the specification automaton can be seen as a sequence of states $q_0 \cdot q_1 \cdot \ldots \cdot q_t \cdot \ldots$. It indicates that, for each timestamp $t \in \mathbb{N}^*$, the automaton is in the state q_t[3]. In a decentralized system, a component receives only local observations and does not necessarily have enough information to determine the state at a given timestamp. Typically, when sufficient information is shared between various components, it is possible to know the state q_t that is reached in the automaton at t (we say that the state q_t has been found, in such a case). The aim of the EHE is to construct a data structure which follows the current state of an automaton, and in case of partial information, tracks the possible states the automaton can be in. For that purpose, we need to ensure strong eventual consistency in determining the state q_t of the execution of an automaton. That is, after two different monitors share their EHE, they should both be able to find q_t for t (if there exists enough information to infer the global state), or if not enough information is available, they both find no state at all.

The Execution History Encoding (EHE) is a data structure designed to encode an execution of an automaton using boolean expressions while accounting for partial observations. An Execution History Encoding of the execution of an automaton $\mathcal{A}$ is

[3] We note that in the case of RV, traces are typically finite.

a partial function $\mathcal{I} : \mathbb{N} \times Q \rightarrow \mathit{Expr}_{\mathit{Atoms}}$. Intuitively, for a given execution, an EHE encodes the conditions to be in a state at a given timestamp as an expression in $\mathit{Expr}_{\mathit{Atoms}}$.

Analyzing the Cost of Monitoring Algorithms. The EHE can be used to abstract away the behavior of a monitoring algorithm. We can leverage it to compare decentralized monitoring algorithms in terms of computation, communication, and memory overhead.

We first express the size of the EHE according to the information delay. The information delay δ_t is the number of timestamps needed to reach a new known state from an existing known state. That is, it is the number of timestamps in the EHE storing partial information without determining a known state. Information delay is a runtime measure, as it depends on the updates done to the EHE as it evolves with time. We use $\mathrm{S}(t)$ to denote the size of an expression in the EHE at t timestamps after a known state. As such to reach a given state, we require a previous expression (i.e., $\mathrm{S}(t-1)$), and add the label of a given transition (of maximum size L). In the worst-case, the automaton is a fully connected graph, a state can be reached from all other states (including itself). Hence, we require the disjunction of $|Q|$ such expressions. The recurrence relation is given by: $\mathrm{S}(t) = |Q| \times (\mathrm{S}(t-1) + L)$. $\mathrm{S}(t)$ is thus a geometric series of ratio strictly greater than 1. There is a unique expression at a known time stamp and the size of such expression is 1 (since the expression is $\top$). We can then deduce that the size of the expression is exponential in the number of timestamps. An EHE contains $\delta_t \times |Q|$ expressions. In the worst case, its total size is exponential in the number of states. Based on this, we were able to obtain the main parameters (e.g., number of components, depth of the communication network) that affect the algorithms in the form of worst case complexity. Knowing the behavior of the algorithms, one can choose which algorithm to run based on the environment (architectures, networks etc.).

6 Decentralizing the Specifications [17]

Context and Motivations. In this work, we shift the focus to a specification that is decentralized. In a so-called *decentralized specification*, a set of automata represent various properties (and dependencies) for different components of a system.

Contributions. We define the notion of a decentralized specification and its semantics, and the various properties on such specifications, and in particular, we introduce *decentralized monitorability*.

Decentralized Specifications. To decentralize the specification, instead of having one automaton, we have a set of specification automata which make use of a set of monitor labels. We refer to these automata as *monitors*. To each monitor, we associate a component. However, the transition labels of a monitor are expressions restricted to either observations local to the component the monitor is attached to or references to other monitors. This ensures that the monitor is labeled with observations it can locally observe or depend (only) on the verdicts of other monitors. To evaluate a trace as one would on a centralized specification, we require one of the monitors to be a starting point, we refer to that monitor as the *root monitor*.

Semantics. The transition function of the decentralized specification is similar to the centralized automaton with the exception of monitor ids. For monitor ids, the memory stores the verdicts of the related monitors. To evaluate each reference ℓ' in the expression, the remainder of the trace starting from the current event timestamp i is evaluated recursively on the automaton $\mathcal{A}_{\ell'}$ from the initial state $q_{\ell'_0} \in \mathcal{A}_{\ell'}$. Then, the verdict of the monitor is associated with ℓ' in the memory.

Decentralized Monitorability. An important notion to consider when dealing with runtime verification is that of monitorability [22,48]. Monitorability of decentralized specification is recursive, and relies on the inter-dependencies between the various decentralized specifications. To compute monitorability, we first build the monitor dependency set for a given monitor associated with a monitor label. Then, the monitor dependency list for a monitor contains all the references to other monitors across all paths in the given automaton, by examining all the transitions. It can be obtained by a simple traversal of the automaton. Second, we construct the monitor dependency graph, which describes the dependencies between monitors. A sufficient condition for decentralized monitorability can then be decided using the local monitorability of the monitors visited during a traversal of the graph.

7 Tool Implementations

In this section, we overview our tool implementations of the previously presented approaches: DecentMon and THEMIS.

7.1 DecentMon: An OCaml Benchmark for Decentralized Monitoring of LTL Formulae [23]

DecentMon[4] is an implementation, simulating the distributed LTL monitoring algorithms described from Sect. 2 to Sect. 3. It consists of ~2,500 LLOC, written in the functional programming language OCaml. It can be freely downloaded and run from [23]. DecentMon takes as input multiple traces (that can be automatically generated), corresponding to the behavior of a distributed system, and an LTL formula. The LTL formulas used in benchmarks can be either randomly generated or follow Dwyer's specification patterns [16]. Then the formula is monitored against the traces in two different modes:

a) by merging the traces to a single, global trace and then using a "central monitor" for the formula (i.e., all local monitors send their respective events to the central monitor who makes the decisions regarding the trace), and
b) by using the decentralized approaches (i.e., each trace is read by a separate monitor).

DecentMon then outputs a comparison report between the algorithms along several metrics that we designed for decentralized monitoring such as number and size of messages, computational operations, delay induced by communication, balance between monitor computations etc.

[4] https://gricad-gitlab.univ-grenoble-alpes.fr/falconey/decentmon.

We also implemented some benchmarks to evaluate our decentralized monitoring algorithm. For the approach described in Sect. 2, our benchmark experiments show that the advantage of the monitoring algorithm is to monitor with *significantly reduced communication overhead* in comparison with a centralized solution where at any time, t, all n monitors send the observed events to a central decision making point. For the approach described in Sect. 4, our benchmark experiments that our algorithm i) leads to a more lightweight implementation, and ii) outperforms the one in [7] along several decentralized monitoring metrics.

7.2 THEMIS [18]

THEMIS[5] is a framework to facilitate the design, development, and analysis of decentralized monitoring algorithms; developed using Java and AspectJ [38] (~5700 LLOC). It consists of a library and command-line tools. The library provides all necessary building blocks to develop, simulate, instrument, and execute decentralized monitoring algorithms. The command-line tools provide basic functionality to generate traces, execute a monitoring run and execute a full experiment (multiple parameterized runs). The workflow of THEMIS is depicted in Fig. 4.

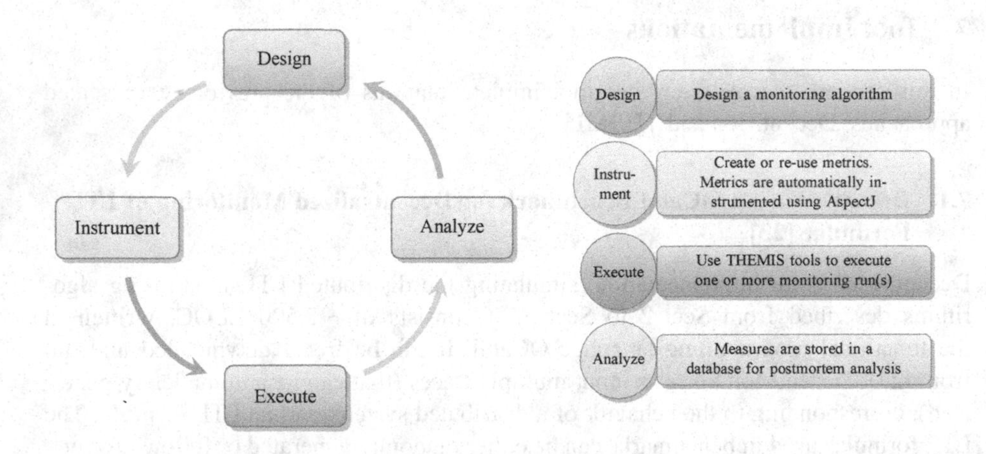

Fig. 4. Overview of THEMIS workflow.

The purpose of THEMIS is to minimize the effort required to design and assess decentralized monitoring algorithms. THEMIS provides an API (Application Programming Interface) for monitoring and necessary data structures to load, encode, store, exchange, and process observations, as well as manipulate specifications and traces. These basic building blocks can be reused or extended to modify existing algorithms or design new more intricate algorithms. To assess the behavior of an algorithm, THEMIS provides a base set of metrics (such as messages exchanged and their size, along with computations performed), but also allows for the definition of new metrics by using the

[5] https://gitlab.inria.fr/monitoring/themis.

API or by writing custom AspectJ instrumentation. These metrics can be used to assess existing algorithms as well as newly developed ones. Once algorithms and metrics are developed, it is possible to use existing tools to perform monitoring runs or full experiments. Experiments are used to define sets of parameters, traces and specifications. An experiment is effectively a folder containing all other necessary files. By bundling everything in one folder, it is possible to share and reproduce the experiment. After running a single run or an experiment, the metrics are stored in a database for postmortem analysis. These can be queried, merged or plotted easily using third-party tools. After completing the analysis, algorithms and metrics can be tuned so as to refine the design as necessary.

We applied THEMIS to the monitoring of smart homes, as described in [19,20].

8 Related Work

In this section, we classify and compare with approaches to decentralized monitoring: monitoring by formula rewriting (Sect. 8), monitoring distributed systems (Sect. 8), fault-tolerant monitoring (Sect. 8), and stream-based monitoring (Sect. 8). We also refer to [33] for a recent overview.

Monitoring by Formula Rewriting. The first class of approaches consists in monitoring by LTL formula rewriting [7,11,50]. Given an LTL formula specifying the system, a monitor will rewrite the formula based on information it has observed or received from other monitors, to generate a formula that has to hold on the next timestamp. Typically a formula is rewritten and simplified until it is equivalent to $\top$ (true) or $\bot$ (false) at which point the algorithm terminates. Another approach [53] extends rewriting to focus on real-time systems. They use Metric Temporal Logic (MTL), which is an extension to LTL with temporal operators. This approach also covers lower bound analysis on monitoring MTL formulae. While these techniques are simple and elegant, rewriting varies significantly during runtime based on observations, thus analyzing the runtime behavior could prove difficult if not unpredictable. For example, when excluding specific syntactic simplification rules, $\mathbf{G}(\top)$ could be rewritten $\top \wedge \mathbf{G}(\top)$ and will keep growing in function of the number of timestamps. To tackle the unpredictability of rewriting LTL formulae, another approach [24] uses automata for monitoring regular languages, and therefore (i) can express richer specifications, and (ii) has predictable runtime behavior. These approaches use a centralized specification to describe the system behavior, they perform decentralized monitoring of a centralized specification, in a system relying on a global clock.

Monitoring Distributed Systems. Approaches to monitoring distributed systems typically consider the problem of detecting global predicates. Global predicate detection [45,46] consists in evaluating predicates on the global state of a distributed system. Approaches performing predicate detection are capable of distributing the evaluation across a distributed system, and evaluate regular predicates which include some temporal logic predicates (such as globally and eventually). The evaluation is done online, and as such can be seen as runtime verification. In [44] the authors extend the approach beyond safety properties to monitor temporal properties in distributed systems. These techniques perform effectively decentralized monitoring of a centralized specification, without assumptions of a global clock.

Fault-Tolerant Monitoring. Another class of research focuses on handling a different problem that arises in distributed systems. In [8], monitors are subject to many faults such as failing to receive correct observations or communicate state with other monitors. Therefore, the problem handled is that of reaching consensus with fault-tolerance and is solved by determining the necessary verdict domain needed to be able to reach a consensus. To remain general, we do not impose the restriction that all monitors must reach the verdict when it is known, as we allow different specifications per monitor. Since we have heterogeneous monitors, we are not particularly interested in consensus. However, for multiple monitors tasked to monitor the same specification, we are interested in strong eventual consistency. We maintain the 3-valued verdict domain and tackle the problem from a different angle by considering the eventual delivery of messages. Similar work [4] extends the MTL approach to deal with failures by modeling knowledge gaps and working on resolving these gaps. We also highlight that the mentioned approaches [4,7,11], and other works [15,51,52] do in effect define separate monitors with different specifications, typically consisting in splitting the formula into subformulas. Then, they describe the collaboration between such monitors. However, when performing *decentralized monitoring of a centralized specification*, approaches primarily focus on presenting one global formula of the system from which they derive multiple specifications. In the approach reported in Sect. 6, we generalize the notions from a centralized to a decentralized specification and separate the problem of generating multiple specifications equivalent to a centralized specification from the monitoring of a decentralized specification.

Stream-Based Monitoring. Specification languages have been developed that monitor synchronous systems as streams [13,14]. In this setting, events are grouped as a stream, and streams are then aggregated by various operators. The output domain extends beyond the Boolean domain and encompasses types. The stream approach to monitoring has the advantage of aggregating types, as such operations such as summing, averaging or pulling statistics across multiple streams is also possible. Stream combination is thus provided by general-purpose functions, which are more complex to analyze than automata. This is similar to complex event processing where RV is a special case [36]. Specification languages such as LOLA [13] even define dependency graphs between various stream information, and have some properties like *well formed*, and *efficiently monitorable* LOLA specifications. The former ensures that dependencies in the trace can be resolved before they are needed, and the latter ensures that the memory requirement is no more than constant with respect to the length of the trace. While streams are general enough to express monitoring, they do not address decentralized monitoring explicitly. As such, there is no explicit assignment of monitors to components and parts of the system, nor consideration of architecture. Furthermore, there is no algorithmic consideration addressing monitoring in a decentralized fashion, even-though some works such as [37] do provide multi-threaded implementations.

9 Conclusions and Future Work

Conclusions. We present a chronological overview of work on the decentralized monitoring of decentralized systems. There are three approaches where monitors differ in their organization and communication strategy, namely orchestration, migration, and choreography. We then present results on the generalization of these approaches into a framework that features (i) a generic data structure for encoding the accumulating knowledge of local monitors and (ii) the notion of decentralized specifications. We present DecentMon, a tool for evaluating the migration and choreography approaches against centralized monitoring along several predefined metrics. We then present THEMIS, a tool for writing customized decentralized monitoring algorithms and metrics.

Perspectives. There are several avenues for future work on decentralized monitoring. First, an important assumption is the existence of global clock. one can consider for instance extending Execution History Encodings so that they rely on vector clocks; as used in [30]. In addition, one can consider augmenting the expressiveness of the specifications being monitored by for instance considering timed specifications or specifications allowing to reason on data. Moreover, while the presented approaches perform verification in that they only aim at detecting specification violation or validation, the question of *reaction* (to specification violations) remains to be studied. For this, one could consider the problem of *runtime enforcement* [22,29,31] in the decentralized setting, as initiated in [34] for temporal logic formulas. Finally, while our latest approach presented in Sect. 5 and Sect. 6 proved to be effective in monitoring smart homes [19], there are many possible case studies where decentralized monitoring can provide benefits in the application domains mentioned in the introduction.

References

1. Barringer, H., Rydeheard, D.E., Havelund, K.: Rule systems for run-time monitoring: from eagle to ruler. J. Log. Comput. **20**(3), 675–706 (2010)
2. Bartocci, E.: Sampling-based decentralized monitoring for networked embedded systems. In: Bortolussi, L., Bujorianu, M.L., Pola, G. (eds.) Proceedings Third International Workshop on Hybrid Autonomous Systems, HAS 2013, Rome, Italy, 17th March 2013. EPTCS, vol. 124, pp. 85–99 (2013)
3. Bartocci, E., Falcone, Y. (eds.): Lectures on Runtime Verification - Introductory and Advanced Topics. LNCS, vol. 10457. Springer, Cham (2018). https://doi.org/10.1007/978-3-319-75632-5
4. Basin, D.A., Klaedtke, F., Zalinescu, E.: Failure-aware runtime verification of distributed systems. In: Harsha, P., Ramalingam, G. (eds.) 35th IARCS Annual Conference on Foundation of Software Technology and Theoretical Computer Science, FSTTCS 2015, Bangalore, India, 16–18 December 2015. LIPIcs, vol. 45, pp. 590–603. Schloss Dagstuhl - Leibniz-Zentrum fuer Informatik (2015)

5. Bauer, A., Falcone, Y.: Decentralised LTL monitoring. Formal Methods Syst. Des. **48**(1–2), 46–93 (2016)
6. Bauer, A., Leucker, M., Schallhart, C.: Monitoring of real-time properties. In: Arun-Kumar, S., Garg, N. (eds.) FSTTCS 2006. LNCS, vol. 4337, pp. 260–272. Springer, Heidelberg (2006). https://doi.org/10.1007/11944836_25
7. Bauer, A., Falcone, Y.: Decentralised LTL monitoring. In: Giannakopoulou, D., Méry, D. (eds.) FM 2012. LNCS, vol. 7436, pp. 85–100. Springer, Heidelberg (2012). https://doi.org/10.1007/978-3-642-32759-9_10
8. Bonakdarpour, B., Fraigniaud, P., Rajsbaum, S., Travers, C.: Challenges in fault-tolerant distributed runtime verification. In: Margaria, T., Steffen, B. (eds.) ISoLA 2016, Part II. LNCS, vol. 9953, pp. 363–370. Springer, Cham (2016). https://doi.org/10.1007/978-3-319-47169-3_27
9. Bose, P.: Power wall. In: Padua, D. (ed.) Encyclopedia of Parallel Computing, pp. 1593–1608. Springer, Boston (2011)
10. Colombo, C., Falcone, Y.: Organising LTL monitors over distributed systems with a global clock. In: Bonakdarpour, B., Smolka, S.A. (eds.) RV 2014. LNCS, vol. 8734, pp. 140–155. Springer, Cham (2014). https://doi.org/10.1007/978-3-319-11164-3_12
11. Colombo, C., Falcone, Y.: Organising LTL monitors over distributed systems with a global clock. Formal Methods Syst. Des. **49**(1–2), 109–158 (2016)
12. Cotsakis, R., St-Onge, D., Beltrame, G.: Decentralized collaborative transport of fabrics using micro-UAVs. In: International Conference on Robotics and Automation, ICRA 2019, Montreal, QC, Canada, 20–24 May 2019, pp. 7734–7740. IEEE (2019)
13. D'Angelo, B., et al.: LOLA: runtime monitoring of synchronous systems. In: 12th International Symposium on Temporal Representation and Reasoning (TIME 2005), Burlington, Vermont, USA, 23–25 June 2005, pp. 166–174. IEEE Computer Society (2005)
14. Decker, N., et al.: Rapidly adjustable non-intrusive online monitoring for multi-core systems. In: Cavalheiro, S., Fiadeiro, J. (eds.) SBMF 2017. LNCS, vol. 10623, pp. 179–196. Springer, Cham (2017). https://doi.org/10.1007/978-3-319-70848-5_12
15. Diekert, V., Muscholl, A.: On distributed monitoring of asynchronous systems. In: Ong, L., de Queiroz, R. (eds.) WoLLIC 2012. LNCS, vol. 7456, pp. 70–84. Springer, Heidelberg (2012). https://doi.org/10.1007/978-3-642-32621-9_5
16. Dwyer, M.B., Avrunin, G.S., Corbett, J.C.: Patterns in property specifications for finite-state verification. In: Boehm, B.W., Garlan, D., Kramer, J. (eds.) Proceedings of the 1999 International Conference on Software Engineering, ICSE 1999, Los Angeles, CA, USA, 16–22 May 1999, pp. 411–420. ACM (1999)
17. El-Hokayem, A., Falcone, Y.: Monitoring decentralized specifications. In: Bultan, T., Sen, K. (eds.) Proceedings of the 26th ACM SIGSOFT International Symposium on Software Testing and Analysis, Santa Barbara, CA, USA, 10–14 July 2017, pp. 125–135. ACM (2017)
18. El-Hokayem, A., Falcone, Y.: THEMIS: a tool for decentralized monitoring algorithms. In: Bultan, T., Sen, K. (eds.) Proceedings of the 26th ACM SIGSOFT International Symposium on Software Testing and Analysis, Santa Barbara, CA, USA, 10–14 July 2017, pp. 372–375. ACM (2017)
19. El-Hokayem, A., Falcone, Y.: Bringing runtime verification home. In: Colombo, C., Leucker, M. (eds.) RV 2018. LNCS, vol. 11237, pp. 222–240. Springer, Cham (2018). https://doi.org/10.1007/978-3-030-03769-7_13
20. El-Hokayem, A., Falcone, Y.: Bringing runtime verification home - a case study on the hierarchical monitoring of smart homes. CoRR abs/1808.05487 (2018)
21. El-Hokayem, A., Falcone, Y.: On the monitoring of decentralized specifications: semantics, properties, analysis, and simulation. ACM Trans. Softw. Eng. Methodol. **29**(1), 1:1–1:57 (2020)

22. Falcone, Y.: You should better enforce than verify. In: Barringer, H., et al. (eds.) RV 2010. LNCS, vol. 6418, pp. 89–105. Springer, Heidelberg (2010). https://doi.org/10.1007/978-3-642-16612-9_9
23. Falcone, Y.: Decentmon website (2021). https://gricad-gitlab.univ-grenoble-alpes.fr/falconey/decentmon
24. Falcone, Y., Cornebize, T., Fernandez, J.-C.: Efficient and generalized decentralized monitoring of regular languages. In: Ábrahám, E., Palamidessi, C. (eds.) FORTE 2014. LNCS, vol. 8461, pp. 66–83. Springer, Heidelberg (2014). https://doi.org/10.1007/978-3-662-43613-4_5
25. Falcone, Y., Fernandez, J.-C., Mounier, L.: Runtime verification of safety-progress properties. In: Bensalem, S., Peled, D.A. (eds.) RV 2009. LNCS, vol. 5779, pp. 40–59. Springer, Heidelberg (2009). https://doi.org/10.1007/978-3-642-04694-0_4
26. Falcone, Y., Fernandez, J., Mounier, L.: What can you verify and enforce at runtime? Int. J. Softw. Tools Technol. Transf. **14**(3), 349–382 (2012)
27. Falcone, Y., Havelund, K., Reger, G.: A tutorial on runtime verification. In: Broy, M., Peled, D.A., Kalus, G. (eds.) Engineering Dependable Software Systems, NATO Science for Peace and Security Series, D: Information and Communication Security, vol. 34, pp. 141–175. IOS Press (2013)
28. Falcone, Y., Krstić, S., Reger, G., Traytel, D.: A taxonomy for classifying runtime verification tools. Int. J. Softw. Tools Technol. Transfer **23**(2), 255–284 (2021). https://doi.org/10.1007/s10009-021-00609-z
29. Falcone, Y., Mariani, L., Rollet, A., Saha, S.: Runtime failure prevention and reaction. In: Bartocci, E., Falcone, Y. (eds.) Lectures on Runtime Verification. LNCS, vol. 10457, pp. 103–134. Springer, Cham (2018). https://doi.org/10.1007/978-3-319-75632-5_4
30. Falcone, Y., Nazarpour, H., Bensalem, S., Bozga, M.: Monitoring distributed component-based systems. In: Salaün, G., Wijs, A. (eds.) FACS 2021. LNCS, vol. 13077, pp. 153–173. Springer, Cham (2021). https://doi.org/10.1007/978-3-030-90636-8_9
31. Falcone, Y., Pinisetty, S.: On the runtime enforcement of timed properties. In: Finkbeiner, B., Mariani, L. (eds.) RV 2019. LNCS, vol. 11757, pp. 48–69. Springer, Cham (2019). https://doi.org/10.1007/978-3-030-32079-9_4
32. Francalanza, A., Gauci, A., Pace, G.J.: Distributed system contract monitoring. J. Log. Algebr. Program. **82**(5–7), 186–215 (2013)
33. Francalanza, A., Pérez, J.A., Sánchez, C.: Runtime verification for decentralised and distributed systems. In: Bartocci and Falcone [3], pp. 176–210
34. Gallay, F., Falcone, Y.: Decentralized LTL enforcement. In: Ganty, P., Bresolin, D. (eds.) Proceedings 12th International Symposium on Games, Automata, Logics, and Formal Verification, GandALF 2021, Padua, Italy, 20–22 September 2021. EPTCS, vol. 346, pp. 135–151 (2021). https://doi.org/10.4204/EPTCS.346.9
35. Gunzert, M., Nägele, A.: Component-based development and verification of safety critical software for a brake-by-wire system with synchronous software components. In: International Symposium on SE for Parallel and Distributed Systems (PDSE), p. 134. IEEE (1999)
36. Hallé, S.: When RV meets CEP. In: Falcone, Y., Sánchez, C. (eds.) RV 2016. LNCS, vol. 10012, pp. 68–91. Springer, Cham (2016). https://doi.org/10.1007/978-3-319-46982-9_6
37. Hallé, S., Khoury, R., Gaboury, S.: Event stream processing with multiple threads. In: Lahiri, S., Reger, G. (eds.) RV 2017. LNCS, vol. 10548, pp. 359–369. Springer, Cham (2017). https://doi.org/10.1007/978-3-319-67531-2_22
38. Kiczales, G., Hilsdale, E., Hugunin, J., Kersten, M., Palm, J., Griswold, W.G.: An overview of AspectJ. In: Knudsen, J.L. (ed.) ECOOP 2001. LNCS, vol. 2072, pp. 327–354. Springer, Heidelberg (2001). https://doi.org/10.1007/3-540-45337-7_18
39. Lichtenstein, O., Pnueli, A., Zuck, L.: The glory of the past. In: Parikh, R. (ed.) Logic of Programs 1985. LNCS, vol. 193, pp. 196–218. Springer, Heidelberg (1985). https://doi.org/10.1007/3-540-15648-8_16

40. Lynch, W.C.: Computer systems: reliable full-duplex file transmission over half-duplex telephone line. Commun. ACM **11**(6), 407–410 (1968)
41. Manna, Z., Pnueli, A.: The Temporal Logic of Reactive and Concurrent Systems. Springer, New York (1992). https://doi.org/10.1007/978-1-4612-0931-7
42. Mayya, S., Pierpaoli, P., Egerstedt, M.: Voluntary retreat for decentralized interference reduction in robot swarms. In: International Conference on Robotics and Automation, ICRA 2019, Montreal, QC, Canada, 20–24 May 2019, pp. 9667–9673. IEEE (2019)
43. Miller, S.P., Whalen, M.W., Cofer, D.D.: Software model checking takes off. Commun. ACM **53**, 58–64 (2010)
44. Mostafa, M., Bonakdarpour, B.: Decentralized runtime verification of LTL specifications in distributed systems. In: 2015 IEEE International Parallel and Distributed Processing Symposium, IPDPS 2015, pp. 494–503. IEEE Computer Society (2015)
45. Natarajan, A., Chauhan, H., Mittal, N., Garg, V.K.: Efficient abstraction algorithms for predicate detection. Theor. Comput. Sci. **688**, 24–48 (2017)
46. Ogale, V.A., Garg, V.K.: Detecting temporal logic predicates on distributed computations. In: Pelc, A. (ed.) DISC 2007. LNCS, vol. 4731, pp. 420–434. Springer, Heidelberg (2007). https://doi.org/10.1007/978-3-540-75142-7_32
47. Pnueli, A.: The temporal logic of programs. In: Proceedings of the 18th Annual Symposium on Foundations of Computer Science, SFCS 1977, pp. 46–57. IEEE Computer Society (1977)
48. Pnueli, A., Zaks, A.: PSL model checking and run-time verification via testers. In: Misra, J., Nipkow, T., Sekerinski, E. (eds.) FM 2006. LNCS, vol. 4085, pp. 573–586. Springer, Heidelberg (2006). https://doi.org/10.1007/11813040_38
49. Pop, T., Pop, P., Eles, P., Peng, Z., Andrei, A.: Timing analysis of the FlexRay communication protocol. Real-Time Syst. **39**, 205–235 (2008)
50. Rosu, G., Havelund, K.: Rewriting-based techniques for runtime verification. Autom. Softw. Eng. **12**(2), 151–197 (2005)
51. Scheffel, T., Schmitz, M.: Three-valued asynchronous distributed runtime verification. In: Twelfth ACM/IEEE International Conference on Formal Methods and Models for Codesign, MEMOCODE 2014, Lausanne, Switzerland, 19–21 October 2014, pp. 52–61. IEEE (2014)
52. Sen, K., Vardhan, A., Agha, G., Rosu, G.: Efficient decentralized monitoring of safety in distributed systems. In: Finkelstein, A., Estublier, J., Rosenblum, D.S. (eds.) 26th International Conference on Software Engineering (ICSE 2004), Edinburgh, United Kingdom, 23–28 May 2004, pp. 418–427. IEEE Computer Society (2004)
53. Thati, P., Rosu, G.: Monitoring algorithms for metric temporal logic specifications. Electron. Notes Theor. Comput. Sci. **113**, 145–162 (2005)

Roles and Responsibilities for a Predictable Update Process – A Position Paper

Astrid Rakow(✉) and Janis Kröger

Carl von Ossietzky Universität Oldenburg, Oldenburg, Germany
{a.rakow,janis.kroeger}@uni-oldenburg.de

Abstract. In contrast to consumer electronics, remotely updating safety critical systems is in its beginnings. Such updates pose the additional challenge of keeping the system safe. Unavailability or degraded performance/functionality can itself be safety critical. Since the update process consumes resources, the installation process of an update can hence endanger system safety. In this paper we argue that contracts assigning responsibilities to the stakeholders as well as assumptions and guarantees regarding timing and resources are necessary to avoid unexpected system degradation. We outline our vision of employing formal methods to check at the back-end whether an update schedule exists and we identify where future research is needed to support this venture.

Keywords: Update process · Contracts · Stakeholder · System safety

1 Introduction

There certainly is a trend towards updating safety critical systems (SCS) in the field: Pioneering car manufacturers like Tesla or BMW sell remotely updatable cars and more will follow [10,16]. Already in 2018, Tesla deployed an over-the-air (OTA) software update to fix their braking system [20]. In the avionics domain a first remote on-wing update has successfully been performed in January 2021 [23]. But other domains like maritime and industrial systems are more hesitant to welcome cyber-physical systems (CPS), not to mention remotely updatable CPS. For instance, the currently well accepted standard IEC 61131 [2] for hard- and software of industrial control systems does not even provide a concept of updates. The new standard IEC 61499 [3] introduces the concept of management/deployment channel. On the other hand, vendors in the automotive domain advertise OTA updates to customers as a convenient way to be up to date with new regulatory standards, to receive safety improvements and fixes as well as a way to optional equipment features [5]. Clearly, the vendors themselves have a strong incentive to perform OTA updates, as it is a flexible mean to reduce the

This work has been funded by the *Federal Ministry of Education and Research* (BMBF) as part of *Step-Up!CPS* (reference no. 01IS18080B).

A. Nouri et al. (Eds.): VECoS 2021, LNCS 13187, pp. 17–26, 2022.
https://doi.org/10.1007/978-3-030-98850-0_2

number of system variants in the field, which eases the burden of supporting all deployed system variants.

The importance of a predictable update process is immanent for real-time safety critical systems like an airbag controller, an emergency vehicle or a chemical plant. Taking safety precautions hinges on the predictability of phases where the system will be unavailable or will provide only degraded functionalities. In our opinion it is necessary to contractually specify responsibilities of the involved stakeholders to make the update process more predictable, since the stakeholders can influence the environment within which the update takes place. We explicate this idea by structuring the update process into phases as building blocks. We then assign responsibilities to the stakeholders via so-called stakeholder contracts and sketch how formal contracts may be employed to specify resource and timing aspects of the update phases. For an update process built of these phases, a virtual integration test (VIT) can be used to check whether the update will be installed in time and whether the system performs during the update as specified.

Outline. In Sect. 2 we present the state of the art and introduce the preliminaries in Sect. 3. We present an overview of the update phases in Sect. 4 and discuss the stakeholder responsibilities in Sect. 5. In Sect. 6 we introduce the contracts of the system and of the update, and we exemplify how a VIT can be used to establish that the stakeholder contract is guaranteed. We conclude in Sect. 7.

2 State of the Art

In this paper we consider remote software updates of a system in the field. These updates may be offline, i.e., the program is stopped and then restarts in the new version, or online, i.e., a dynamic software update (DSU). Since during a DSU the system continues to provide its services, it seems more appealing but at the same time more challenging –in particular when degradation may be safety critical. Surveys of the works on DSU are given in e.g. [21,24]. Miedes et al. [21] compile a list of desirable requirements and goals from the DSU literature and give an overview of influential papers on DSU itself and of papers dealing with issues complementary to DSU. Finally, they summarise important concepts, issues and techniques. In his dissertation [24] de Pina lists challenges for DSU and defines goals that a DSU solution should achieve. He compares and classifies the state of the art with respect to concepts and techniques of DSU. Dominant research topics for the more general topic of updates in the field are firmware updates (e.g. [14]) and security (e.g. [12]). We propose an approach to schedule an update process with a certain performance profile. We formulate contractual obligations that include the stakeholder. Our considerations do not focus on a particular technique. They moreover focus on the update process rather than on the update. We expect that many systems will use offline as well as dynamic updates depending on the risk that the update process poses to system safety.

The survey [19] reviews works on the use of formal methods to establish DSU correctness and discusses notions of update correctness. Our approach specifies guarantees regarding the timing of the update process and regarding the system performance during the update process. These guarantees can be considered as a correctness requirement of the update process. We thereby extend the focus of update correctness to update process correctness. Whereas Gupta [11] suggested a notion of update correctness according to which the updated system *eventually* has to behave as if the update had been on the system right from the start, establishing a time bound for the update process is inevitably necessary. Moreover, there are formal approaches tackling the problem of transitioning from the current version of a system to a new version. For example [4] presents a generic formal model using correct-by-construction stepwise refinement and proof-based formal methods, while the authors of [22] define the correctness criteria for a dynamic controller update and synthesise a controller guiding the current system to a safe state where the update will eventually occur.

Hayden et al. presented in [13] an approach to ensuring at the development that a dynamically updated program will behave correctly. Similarly, we are concerned with the question of how it can be ensured at design time that the update process behaves well. The above works on formal update correctness study the relation of the old and the new version, while we reason about the update process and its dependencies to the stakeholders. We envision to specify formal contracts for the system and the update (phases). The formal foundation of these contracts is the contract based design methodology [9]. Moreover, stakeholder contracts formulate obligations for the stakeholder to increase the predictability of update process. As a consequence an update provider can develop more reliable update process schedules and users are more reliably informed about the system performance during these schedules. Therefore, we structure the update process into phases. Similar phases can be found e.g. in [27]. There the authors focus on schedulability analysis for real-time systems. While their maxim is to realise DSUs that do not interfere with the real-time tasks, we allow that an update is installed offline, since we consider the wider class of systems that become unsafe due to unavailability or degradation.

3 Preliminaries

We consider the update process of *safety critical systems*, i.e., systems whose failure can result in loss of life or significant damage to the environment [15]. More precisely, we are concerned with remote software updates of (embedded) systems *in the field*, that is after deployment at the user's site.

We distinguish three stakeholders: the update developer, the update provider and the user. The *user* is at the same site as the target system so that he can e.g. plug in and unplug devices in the periphery of the system. The *update provider* decides what compilation of updates is transferred to the target system and thus controls the number of variants in the field. We assume that the update provider is also the *system integrator* knowing the overall system as an integration of its parts. The *update developer* knows part of the system in detail and develops an update for this part. She has only limited knowledge of the overall system.

We use the term *front-end* to refer to the system's site, while we use the term *back-end* to refer to the sites of the update provider and update developers. We use the term *user functionality* to refer to the system's front-end functionality that is provided to the user.

We consider systems build of *components* where only some components will be updated. Very generally, a component M is an open system, i.e., it has some inputs that are provided by its environment, and it generates some outputs. Components can be composed to build a new component.

An *assume-guarantee contract* is a tuple $C = (A, G)$ where A specifies the legal working environment of a component M and G specifies the effect of M, i.e. A is a property that the environment must satisfy and G is a property that the component M must satisfy. A contract defined this way expresses that, if M is placed in an environment as described by A, M will behave as described by G. Each component of a system can be annotated with contracts. Based on these contracts one can perform a *virtual integration test* (VIT). Virtual integration means to perform integration activities virtually before they are finally carried out on the real system [26]. The composition $C_1 \otimes C_2$ of the two contracts C_1 and C_2 corresponds to a contract of a system that is composed of two components K_1 and K_2 with the respective contracts C_1 and C_2, which should satisfy: Composing K_1 and K_2 yields an implementation of $C_1 \otimes C_2$ and any environment of $C_1 \otimes C_2$, when composed with an implementation of C_1, should yield a valid environment of C_2 and vice-versa [9].

4 Overview of the Update Phases

We now introduce the update phases that seamlessly cover the update process from the time an update is available at an update provider till the time when the update installation is completed (cf. Fig. 1). Our vision is that they constitute the building blocks of time and performance management of the update process. Each phase of a *normal* update gets an upper time limit and a performance profile assigned.

A normal update proceeds according to plan, but it can subsume unsuccessful attempts including roll-backs. In contrast, *severely failed* updates require that a fix has to be unexpectedly developed after the failure occurred (cf. Sect. 4.1). Normal phases represent blocks of known duration and performance characteristics. A chain of normal phases hence corresponds to an update schedule with a system performance profile and stakeholder duties (cf. Sect. 5).

4.1 The Update Phases

The *Update Transmission Phase* starts when the update is available at the update provider and ends with its successful transmission. The *Pending Update Phase* starts when the update is available on the target system and ends when the update installation on the target system is started. It may have a considerable extent, if the system is waiting for completion of its current mission or if

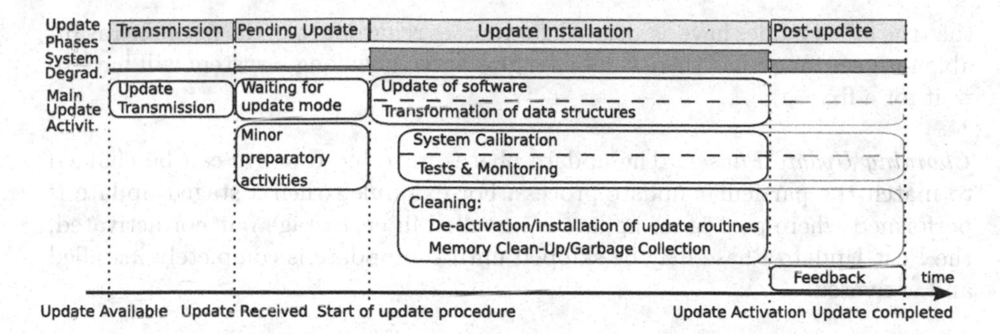

Fig. 1. Overview of phases of a normal update process

the update installation is started manually. The *Update Installation Phase* starts with the installation of the update and ends with the activation of the installed update or a transition into a failed update mode. Accompanying tests, calibration and cleaning may take place. For SCS, it is especially important that all safety tests have been passed before the update is activated. Often the system provides during this phase only limited or no user functionality either as a safety measure or since the installation activities consume so much of the resources. The *Post-Update Phase* starts with the activation of the installed update and ends when the system is fully operational. It is characterised by increased monitoring, tests, calibration and clean up. System calibration adapts the system to the user's preferences and characteristics in the field, while tests and monitoring activities aim to provide feedback for further improvements. This phase may require increased data transmission capacities.

We assume that usually the greatest system degradation occurs during the Update Installation Phase itself and some degradation during the Post Update Phase (cf. Fig. 1). It certainly depends on the particular system and the update how severely the update activities influence the front-end functionalities.

Limiting the Time of the Post-Update Phase Some activities of the Post-Update Phase may only be triggered by a certain usage context in the field, leading to an unexpected degradation that can be safety critical. We hence propose, that the user and the update provider contractually specify what update contexts the update provider may request from user to establish during the Post Update Phase.

Severely Failed Updates. In case an update installation fails so severely that no roll-back can be performed and a dedicated fix has to be developed, the system transitions into the *Severely Failed Update Phase.* It starts with the activation of a mode of degraded performance and ends when the system transitions back to its nominal mode (cf. Sect. 6), which is achieved by a subsequent (repair) update. During this phase the system usually provides only degraded availability, functionality or performance, because the system is in a corrupted intermediate state and resources are allocated to document, diagnose and bridge the update failure. While we assume that the failed modes have associated guarantees regarding e.g. the resources available for user functions, there can be no guarantee how long a system will have to wait for a fix.

Chaining Update Phases. The update phases introduced above can be chained to match the particular update process. For example, when a staged update is performed where part of an update is installed in each stage but not activated, the Post-Update Phase may be skipped until the update is completely installed and activated.

5 Stakeholder Contracts

The stakeholder contracts (i) make environmental and organisational prerequisites of the update process explicit and (ii) specify what rights and responsibilities the stakeholders have. As a consequence an update provider can plan a schedule of an update process more easily, while a user knows in advance what the system performance will be like. The update provider and the user agree on the terms of the update process. The user gets mainly responsible for establishing certain conditions in the system's environment while the update provider is foremost responsible for installing the updates within the specified time and performance profile. The update provider plans the update process as a chain of update phases. For each phase there are assume-guarantee contracts for the system and the update (cf. Sect. 6). Together they specify how the update process on the target system will behave – but only if the stakeholders take care of establishing the update process's prerequisites (cf. (i)). Thus the chain of update phases corresponds to a chain of contracts, from which the update provider can derive the duration and the performance profile of the update process and check whether this satisfies the stakeholder contract.

While the system contract and the update contract are *formal contracts*, the stakeholder contracts are rather a kind of legal contract and may be part of the sales contract. In the following we outline the stakeholder contracts for the update phases. During *Update Transmission* the update provider is responsible for making the update available. His responsibility includes e.g. that the update bundles are of an appropriate size and that there are sufficiently many update servers in place. The user guarantees that she enables the system to retrieve updates – either by connecting the system to infrastructure so that the system can autonomously retrieve the update or by transferring the received update to the system. Since the transmission medium is usually not in the control of any stakeholder, the transmission time and losses due to the transmission medium will be conservatively approximated. For the *Pending Update Phase*, the user agrees to let the system switch to an *update mode* on a regular basis (e.g. when it is predictable that the system will not be used) or within an agreed time interval after an update trigger (e.g. invitation/demand to update). Note, that hence a push update is possible. For the *Update Installation Phase*, the user agrees that the system stays in the update mode for a certain duration (e.g. 1 h per week). He is responsible for establishing the agreed environmental conditions for a successful installation of the update (e.g. internet access, power supply). The update provider guarantees that necessary updates will always request environmental conditions that can be established by all eligible users. For the *Post-Update Phase*, the users are made responsible for providing the required access to a transmission medium, so that collected data can be transferred from the system to the update provider, Also, the environmental test/trigger contexts, that may be required (cf. Sect. 4.1) for context dependent tests and calibrations have to be established by the users. The update provider guarantees that the requested environmental contexts can be established by all eligible users. For the *Severely Failed Update Phase*, the update provider is responsible for notifying the user of the implied system degradation, and she is responsible for fixing the problem, although she will usually delegate this responsibility to the update developer. The user is responsible for using the system only in a safe way taking the degraded performance into account.

6 System and Update Contracts

In addition to the stakeholder contracts, we envision formal contracts for the update and the target system. An *update contract* specifies what system resources, or rather *services*, the update assumes to be available on the target system (for e.g. running tests, installation) and it specifies guarantees about the update's service utilisation. A *system contract* specifies what services are guaranteed by the system and what it assumes of its environment, e.g. internet access, rates of input signals etc. So, the update provider first has to decide on an *update bundle* from the set of possibly interdependent software component updates [8]. Then he can check via a VIT whether a successful update process is guaranteed, i.e. he examines whether the composition of the update (bundle) contract and the system contract implies the times and performance profiles of the stakeholder contracts. If the VIT is passed and given the update, system and stakeholders satisfy their contracts, it is formally proven that the update process will be on time and the system will perform as promised during the update.

Contracts and Modes. System contracts specify what the performance of the user functionality is and what services are available in each update phase. In order to link this contractually specified behaviour to the behaviour of the system, we use the concept of *mode-based contracts* [18] and consider our phases as *modes* (cf. Fig. 2). Modes partition a system's state set. A mode contract allows to specify that the system has to satisfy a mode dependent contract while its state is in mode m. Different from [18], we assume that modes are hierarchically structured, so that we can define the update phases in terms of the system's modes.

Services and Contracts. Both, system and update contracts, specify functional behaviour as well as resource usage. For these we envision to use the service concept as in the ARAMiS projects [1] for layered architectures as e.g. [28]. A *service* describes abstractly the functionality that is provided by a given hardware and software system that can be used to run software, e.g. a middleware

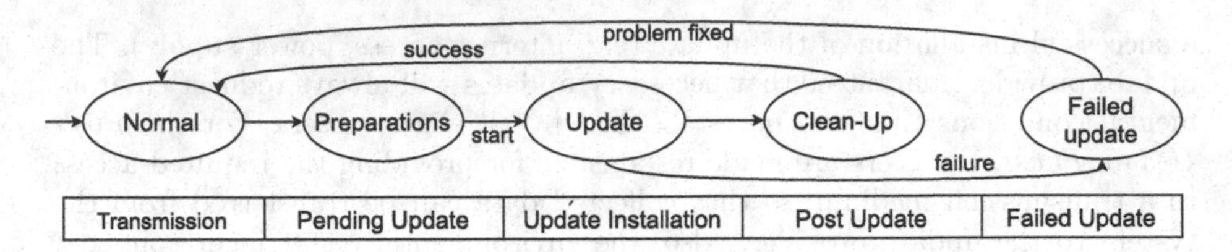

Fig. 2. A coarse example of a mode model and phases

component may require a read or write service of the technical layer. These services can be specified via assume-guarantee contracts, e.g. we can specify the guaranteed performance for an assumed input characteristics, and the contracts can also capture interdependencies to other services [6,7]. Since the services may compete for shared resources like a bus or a CPU, it has to be checked whether a global schedule exists when services are composed. To ease this task segregation properties are exploited [25,29]. We envision a segregation of user functionality from the update process. For system and update contracts, the service contracts of ARAMiS will have to be extended to mode contracts as in [18]. First steps towards this goal have been made [17], but parts of the works on service contracts are still unpublished and others are even work in progress. Moreover, we need a stronger support of data dependent service contracts.

Let us now illustrate via a small scenario how an update process could be like when using stakeholder, update and system contracts. The update provider plans the update process in terms of a sequence of update phases. Let us say the update provider wants to install a safety critical update within one month. He specifies an update bundle to update a fleet of cars. He then derives how long it will take to transmit the bundle, how long the update may be pending, how long the installation will take etc. All of this information is derived from the (update, system and stakeholder) contracts of the respective phases. After he finds out that the transmission will take too much time, he decides to do a two staged update. A first bundle will be installed, then a second bundle will be installed, whose selection depends on feedback from the target system after the first bundle's installation. That way the bundles are reduced in size and tailored to the system. The update provider then verifies by a VIT that the staged update will be completed within one month and that the update does not cause the system to degrade more than allowed. After also this test is successfully completed, he makes the update available to the user.

7 Conclusions and Future Challenges

In this paper we suggest dividing the update process into phases. We advocate to assign responsibilities to the different stakeholders in form of stakeholder contracts, which make environmental and organisational prerequisites of the update process as well as rights and responsibilities of the stakeholders explicit.

We outline our vision of using mode based, data dependent service contracts as the formal foundation for the update and system contracts. While service contracts are developed within the ARAMiS project [1], we consider mode-based data-dependent service contracts as future work.

Based on the system, update and stakeholder contracts, it can be proven via a VIT that the update will be in time and as performant as specified. So users can rely on a more predictable system performance during the update while the update provider can rely on guaranteed update time windows to develop the system further.

References

1. ARAMiS II (2019). https://www.aramis2.org
2. 65B, T.S.: IEC 61131 Programmable controllers (2003)
3. 65B, T.S.: IEC 61499 Function Blocks (2012)
4. Babin, G., Ait-Ameur, Y., Pantel, M.: Correct instantiation of a system reconfiguration pattern: a proof and refinement-based approach. In: 2016 IEEE 17th International Symposium on High Assurance Systems Engineering (HASE), pp. 31–38 (2016). https://doi.org/10.1109/HASE.2016.47
5. Barnwell, D.: Your guid to the ins and outs of BMW software updates. https://www.bmw.com/en/innovation/bmw-software-update.html. Accessed 15 Mar 2021
6. Bauer, B., et al.: E3.1 Partitioning of Functionality. ARAMIS II Project
7. Baumgart, A., et al.: Architecture Modeling. Technical report, OFFIS (2011)
8. Bebawy, Y., et al.: Incremental contract-based verification of software updates for safety-critical cyber-physical systems. In: 2020 International Conference on Computational Science and Computational Intelligence (CSCI), 2020 (2020)
9. Benveniste, A., et al.: Contracts for System Design. Foundations and Trends® in Electronic Design Automation **12**(2–3), 124–400 (2018)
10. Future, M.R.: Global Automotive Over-The-Air (OTA) Updates Market Research Report. https://www.marketresearchfuture.com/reports/automotive-over-the-air-updates-market-7606. Accessed 15 Mar 2021
11. Gupta, D., Jalote, P., Barua, G.: A Formal framework for on-line software version change. IEEE Trans. Softw. Eng. **22**(2), 120–131 (1996)
12. Halder, S., Ghosal, A., Conti, M.: Secure over-the-air software updates in connected vehicles: a survey. Comput. Netw. **178**, 107343 (2020)
13. Hayden, C.M., Magill, S., Hicks, M., Foster, N., Foster, J.S.: Specifying and Verifying the Correctness of Dynamic Software Updates. In: Joshi, R., Müller, P., Podelski, A. (eds.) VSTTE 2012. LNCS, vol. 7152, pp. 278–293. Springer, Heidelberg (2012). https://doi.org/10.1007/978-3-642-27705-4_22
14. Jain, N., Mali, S.G., Kulkarni, S.: Infield firmware update: challenges and solutions. In: 2016 International Conference on Communication and Signal Processing (ICCSP), pp. 1232–1236 (2016)
15. Knight, J.: Safety Critical Systems: Challenges and Directions. In: Proceedings of the 24th International Conference on Software Engineering. ICSE 2002. pp. 547–550 (2002)
16. Koegel, M., Wolf, M.: Auto update – safe and secure over-the-air (SOTA) software update for advanced driving assistance systems. In: Isermann, R. (ed.) Fahrerassistenzsysteme 2016, pp. 119–134. Springer, Wiesbaden (2018). https://doi.org/10.1007/978-3-658-21444-9_9

17. Kröger, J., Koopmann, B., Stierand, I., Tabassam, N., Fränzle, M.: Handling of operating modes in contract-based timing specifications. In: Nouri, A., et al. (eds.) VECoS 2021. LNCS, vol. 13187, pp. 59–74. Springer, Cham (2022)
18. Kugele, S., Marmsoler, D., Mata, N., Werther, K.: Verification of component architectures using mode-based contracts. In: 2016 ACM/IEEE International Conference on Formal Methods and Models for System Design (MEMOCODE), pp. 133–142 (2016)
19. Lounas, R., Mezghiche, M., Lanet, J.: Formal methods in dynamic software updating: a survey. Int. J. Critical Comput. Syst. **9**(1–2), 76–114 (2019)
20. Marshall, A.: Tesla's Quick Fix for Its Braking System Came From the Ether (2018). https://www.wired.com/story/tesla-model3-braking-software-update-consumer-reports. Accessed 15 Mar 2021
21. Miedes, E., Muñoz-Escoí, F.: A Survey about Dynamic Software Updating. Instituto Universitario Mixto Tecnologico de Informatica, Universitat Politecnica de Valencia, Campus de Vera s/n 46022 (2012)
22. Nahabedian, L., Braberman, V., D'Ippolito, N., Honiden, S., Kramer, J., Tei, K., Uchitel, S.: Dynamic update of discrete event controllers. IEEE Trans. Softw. Eng. **46**(11), 1220–1240 (2020). https://doi.org/10.1109/TSE.2018.2876843
23. Network, A.W.: MRO News Briefs, 17–23 January, 2021. https://aviationweek.com/mro/mro-news-briefs-jan-17-23-2021. Accessed 02 Mar 2021
24. de Pina, L.: Practical Dynamic Software Updating. Ph.D. thesis, University of Lisbon, Portugal (2016)
25. Reinkemeier, P., Benveniste, A., Damm, W., Stierand, I.: Contracts for Schedulability Analysis. In: Sankaranarayanan, S., Vicario, E. (eds.) FORMATS 2015. LNCS, vol. 9268, pp. 270–287. Springer, Cham (2015). https://doi.org/10.1007/978-3-319-22975-1_18
26. Rhanoui, M., Asri, B.: A contractual specification of functional and non-functional requirements of domain-specific components. Int. J. Comput. Sci. Issues **11**, 172–181 (2014)
27. Ribeiro, L.B., Baunach, M.: Towards dynamically composed real-time embedded systems. In: Logistik und Echtzeit. I, pp. 11–20. Springer, Heidelberg (2017). https://doi.org/10.1007/978-3-662-55785-3_2
28. Staron, M.: AUTOSAR (AUTomotive Open System ARchitecture). In: Automotive Software Architectures, pp. 97–136. Springer, Cham (2021). https://doi.org/10.1007/978-3-030-65939-4_5
29. Stierand, I., Reinkemeier, P., Bhaduri, P.: Virtual integration of real-time systems based on resource segregation abstraction. In: Legay, A., Bozga, M. (eds.) FORMATS 2014. LNCS, vol. 8711, pp. 206–221. Springer, Cham (2014). https://doi.org/10.1007/978-3-319-10512-3_15

Hybrid Parallel Model Checking of Hybrid LTL on Hybrid State Space Representation

Kais Klai[1], Chiheb Ameur Abid[2,3](✉), Jaime Arias[1], and Sami Evangelista[1]

[1] University of Sorbonne Paris Nord, LIPN, CNRS UMR 7030, Villetaneuse, France
{klai,arias,evangelista}@lipn.univ-paris13.fr

[2] Faculty of Sciences of Tunis, University of Tunis El Manar, 2092 Tunis, Tunisia
chiheb.abid@fst.utm.tn

[3] Mediatron Lab, SupCom, University of Carthage, Tunis, Tunisia

Abstract. In this paper, we propose a hybrid parallel model checking algorithm for both shared and distributed memory architectures. The model checking is performed simultaneously with a parallel construction of system state space by distributed multi-core machines. The representation of the system's state space is a hybrid graph called Symbolic Observation Graph (SOG), which combines the symbolic representation of its nodes (sets of single states) and the explicit representation of its arcs. The SOG is adapted to allow the preservation of both state and event-based LTL formulae (hybrid LTL), i.e. the atomic propositions involved in the formula to be checked are either state or event-based propositions.

We have implemented the proposed model checker within a C++ prototype and compared our preliminary results to the LTSmin model checker.

Keywords: Decision diagrams · Linear temporal logic · Model checking · Parallel verification

1 Introduction

Model checking [10] has proven to be a major formal verification technique. It is based on an automatic procedure that takes a model M of a system and a formula φ expressing a temporal property, and decides whether the system satisfies the property (denoted by $M \models \varphi$). The automata-based LTL verification decision procedure is reduced to the emptiness check of a synchronized product between two automata A_M and $A_{\neg\varphi}$ (denoted by $A_M \times A_{\neg\varphi}$). A_M represents the state space of the system and $A_{\neg\varphi}$ represents the automaton of the negation of the formula φ to be verified (i.e. accepting all the words that do not satisfy φ). Thus, model checking is based on an exhaustive exploration of the system state space and, consequently, suffers from the state space explosion problem [31].

The system state space can be represented explicitly (i.e. each state/arc of the graph is represented individually) or symbolically (i.e. the set of the reachable states is represented compactly using decision diagram-based techniques).

A. Nouri et al. (Eds.): VECoS 2021, LNCS 13187, pp. 27–42, 2022.
https://doi.org/10.1007/978-3-030-98850-0_3

Hybrid representation of the state space (i.e. an explicit graph where nodes are sets of reachable states encoded symbolically) is also possible, allowing to combine the advantages of both representations. Several approaches (e.g. [5,6,11,15,17–19,21,23,28,30]) have been proposed to cope with the state space explosion problem in order to get a manageable state space and to improve the scalability of the model checking. In addition to techniques for reduction and compression, parallel and distributed-memory processing can be used [2]. The use of distributed processing increases the speed and scalability of model checking by exploiting the cumulative computational power and memory of a cluster of computers. Such approaches have been studied in various contexts leading to different solutions for both symbolic and explicit model checking (e.g. [2–4,14,20]).

A Symbolic Observation Graph (SOG) [18,23] is a graph whose construction is guided by a set of *observable* atomic propositions involved in a formula. These atomic propositions can represent events or actions (event-based SOG [18]), or state-based properties (state-based SOG [23]). The nodes of a SOG are aggregates hiding a set of local states which are equivalent with respect to the observable atomic propositions, and are compactly encoded using Binary Decision Diagram techniques (BDDs) [9]. The arcs of an event-based SOG are exclusively labeled with observable actions. It has been proven that both event and state-based SOGs preserve *stutter-invariant* LTL formulae [18,23]. Moreover, once built for a given LTL formula ϕ_1, the SOG can be reused to check any other LTL formula ϕ_2 involving a subset of the atomic propositions of ϕ_1.

In previous works, we have investigated different approaches to parallelize the SOG construction. In [24,25], we propose different algorithms to benefit from additional speedups and performance improvement in execution time and memory saving. However, in some cases where huge state spaces are involved [1], the model checking does not finish due to lack of memory, or it takes too long.

In this work, we present a distributed model checking technique based on the SOG. It extends the multi-core SOG-based model checker introduced in [1] by allowing the handling of huge state spaces. To achieve this, we propose a hybrid technique that combines parallel (shared memory) and distributed (message passing) construction algorithms [1,27]. Roughly, the construction of a SOG is partitioned over a set of processes which, in turn, distribute the building of their sub-graphs over a set of threads. We thus exploit the strengths of the parallel exploration/construction of the SOG, and distribute the processes in charge of the construction and the verification over multiple machines when a single one (although multi-core) is not sufficient.

In the proposed algorithm, both event- and state-based LTL properties can be expressed, combined, and verified. Here, the event-based and state-based semantics are interchangeable: an event can be encoded as a change in state variables, and likewise one can equip a state with different events to reflect different values of its internal variables. However, converting from one representation to the other often leads to a significant enlargement of the state space. Typically, event-based semantics is adopted to compare systems according to some equivalence or pre-order relation (e.g. [21,29]), while state-based semantics is more suitable to model-checking approaches [16]. Combining both semantics then allows to express properties in a compact and intuitive manner.

The paper is structured as follows. First, we recall in Sect. 2 the notions of Kripke structures and hybrid LTL. Then, in Sect. 3, we introduce the event and state-based SOG. Section 4 describes the main contribution of the paper: a model checker based on the hybrid parallel construction of an event- and state-based SOG. The proposed approach is evaluated and compared to other related works in Sect. 5. Finally, Sect. 6 is dedicated to conclusion and perspectives.

2 Preliminaries

In this paper, we consider hybrid linear-time temporal logic (hybrid LTL) formulae where both state- and event-based atomic propositions can occur. Therefore, we chose to represent the semantics (behavior) of a system by a *Labeled Kripke Structure* (*LKS*). Next, we present their formal definition and semantics.

Definition 1 (Labeled Kripke Structure (LKS)). *Let* AP *be a finite set of atomic propositions and* Act *be a set of actions. An* LKS *over* AP *is a 5-tuple* $\langle \Gamma, Act, L, \rightarrow, s_0 \rangle$ *where:*

- Γ *is a finite set of* states,
- $L : \Gamma \rightarrow 2^{AP}$ *is a* labeling (or interpretation) function,
- $\rightarrow \subseteq \Gamma \times Act \times \Gamma$ *is a* transition relation, *and*
- $s_0 \in \Gamma$ *is the* initial state.

Definition 2 (Hybrid LTL). *Given a set of atomic propositions* AP *and a set of actions* Act, *a* hybrid LTL *formula is defined inductively as follows:*

- *each member of* $AP \cup Act$ *is a formula,*
- *if* ϕ *and* ψ *are hybrid LTL formulae, so are* $\neg\phi$, $\phi \vee \psi$, $X\phi$ *and* $\phi U \psi$.

Other temporal operators, e.g. F (eventually) and G (always) can be derived as follows: $F\phi = true \cup \phi$ and $G\phi = \neg F \neg \phi$.

An interpretation of a hybrid LTL formula is an infinite run $w = s_0 s_1 s_2 \ldots$ (of some *LKS*), assigning to each state s_i a set of atomic propositions and a set of actions that are satisfied within that state. A $p \in AP$ is satisfied by a state s_i if it belongs to its label (i.e. $L(s_i)$), while an action $a \in Act$ is said to be satisfied within a state s_i if it occurs from this state in w (i.e. $(s_i, a, s_{i+1}) \in \rightarrow$). In our case, where a single action can occur at a time (i.e. interleaving model of concurrency), at most one action can be assigned to a state of a run.

We write w^i for the suffix of w starting from s_i. Moreover, we say that $p \in s_i$, for $p \in AP \cup Act$, when p is satisfied by s_i. The hybrid LTL semantics is then defined inductively as follows:

- $w \models p$ iff $p \in s_0$, for $p \in AP \cup Act$,
- $w \models \phi \vee \psi$ iff $w \models \phi$ or $w \models \psi$,
- $w \models \neg\phi$ iff not $w \models \psi$,
- $w \models X\phi$ iff $w^1 \models \phi$, and
- $w \models \phi U \psi$ iff $\exists i \geq 0$ such that $w^i \models \psi$ and $\forall 0 \leq j < i$, $w^j \models \phi$.

Thus, an *LKS* K satisfies a hybrid LTL formula φ, denoted by $K \models \varphi$, iff all its runs satisfy φ.

It is well known that LTL formulae without the *next operator* (X), denoted by $LTL \setminus X$, are invariant under the so-called *stuttering equivalence* [10]. Stuttering occurs when the same atomic propositions hold on two or more consecutive states of a given run. In the next section, we will use this equivalence relation to prove that event- and state-based SOGs preserve hybrid $LTL \setminus X$ properties.

3 Event-Based and State-Based SOG

Symbolic Observation Graph (SOG) [18,23] is an abstraction of the reachability graph of concurrent systems. The construction of a SOG is guided by the set of atomic propositions occurring in the LTL formula to be checked. Such atomic propositions are called *observed*, while the others are *unobserved*. Nodes of the SOG are called *aggregates*, each of them is a set of states encoded efficiently using decision diagram techniques (e.g. LDD [7], a List-implementation of Multiway Decision Diagrams). Despite the exponential theoretical complexity of the size of a SOG (a single state can belong to several aggregates), its size is, in practice, much more reduced than the one of the original reachability graph.

The difference between the event-based and the state-based versions of the SOG ([18] and [23], respectively) is the *aggregation criterion*. In the event-based version, observed atomic propositions correspond to some actions of the system, and aggregates contain states that are connected by unobserved actions. On the other hand, in the state-based version, observed atomic propositions are Boolean state-based conditions, and aggregates regroup states with the same truth values of the observed atomic propositions.

In this section, we present the definition of an **event-state based SOG** which abstracts systems' behavior while preserving hybrid LTL formulae (i.e. both state- and action-based atomic propositions can be used within a same formula). In that sense, the construction of aggregates will depend on both a set of actions and state variables appearing as atomic propositions in the checked formula. Here, systems' behavior will be modeled as Labeled Kripke Structures (*LKS*).

3.1 Revisiting SOG for Hybrid LTL

The adaptation of the SOG to hybrid LTL leads to new aggregation criteria: (1) two states belonging to a same aggregate must have the same truth values of the state-based atomic propositions of the formula; (2) for any state s in the aggregate, any state s' having the same truth values of the atomic propositions as s, and being reachable from s by the occurrence of an unobserved action, belongs necessarily to the same aggregate; and (3) for any state s in the aggregate, any state s' which is reachable from s by the occurrence of an observed action, is not a member of the same aggregate (even if it has the same label as s), unless it is reachable from another state s'' of the aggregate by an unobserved action.

In the following, we present the formal definition of an aggregate and a SOG, according to a given *LKS* and the new aggregation criteria discussed above.

Definition 3 (Event-State Based Aggregate). *Let $\mathcal{K} = \langle \Gamma, Act, L, \rightarrow, s_0 \rangle$ be an LKS over a set of atomic propositions AP, and $Obs \subseteq Act$ be a set of observed actions of $\mathcal{K}$. Then, $UnObs = Act \setminus Obs$ denotes the set of unobserved actions. An aggregate a of $\mathcal{K}$ w.r.t. Obs is a triplet $\langle S, d, l \rangle$ satisfying:*

- *$S \subseteq \Gamma$ where:*
  - $\forall s, s' \in S, L(s) = L(s')$;
  - $\forall s \in S, (\exists (s', u) \in \Gamma \times UnObs \mid L(s') = L(s) \wedge s \xrightarrow{u} s') \Rightarrow s' \in S$;
  - $\forall s \in S, ((\exists (s', o) \in \Gamma \times Obs \mid s \xrightarrow{o} s') \wedge (\nexists (s'', u) \in S \times UnObs \mid L(s'') = L(s') \wedge s'' \xrightarrow{u} s')) \Rightarrow s' \notin S$.
- *$d \in \{\mathtt{true}, \mathtt{false}\}$; $d = \mathtt{true}$ iff S contains a dead state.*
- *$l \in \{\mathtt{true}, \mathtt{false}\}$; $l = \mathtt{true}$ iff S contains an unobserved cycle.*

Before defining event-state based SOGs, let us define the following operations:

- $\mathsf{SAT_{AP}}(S)$: for a set of states $S \subseteq \Gamma$ with the same labels (i.e. such that $L(s) = L(s')$, for any $s, s' \in S$), returns the set of states that are reachable from any state in S by a sequence of unobserved actions, and which have the same value of the atomic propositions as S. It is defined as follows:

$$\mathsf{SAT_{AP}}(S) = \left\{ s'' \in \Gamma \,\middle|\, \begin{array}{l} \exists s \in S, \exists \sigma \in UnObs^*, s \xrightarrow{\sigma} s'' \wedge \\ \forall s' \in \Gamma, \forall \beta \text{ prefix of } \sigma, s \xrightarrow{\beta} s' \Rightarrow L(s) = L(s') \end{array} \right\}$$

- $\mathsf{Out}(a, t)$: returns, for an aggregate $a = \langle S, d, l \rangle$ and action t, the set of states that are reachable from some state in a by firing t. It is defined as follows:

$$\mathsf{Out}(a,t) = \begin{cases} \text{if } t \in Obs & \{s' \in \Gamma \mid \exists s \in S, s \xrightarrow{t} s'\} \\ \text{if } t \in UnObs & \{s' \in \Gamma \mid \exists s \in S, s \xrightarrow{t} s' \wedge L(s) \neq L(s')\} \end{cases}$$

- $\mathsf{Out}_\tau(a)$: returns, for an aggregate a, the set of states whose label is different from the label of any state of a, and which are reachable from some state in a by firing unobserved actions. It is defined as follows:

$$\mathsf{Out}_\tau(a) = \bigcup_{t \in UnObs} Out(a, t)$$

- $\mathsf{Part_{AP}}(S)$: returns, for a set of states $S \subseteq \Gamma$, the set of subsets of S that defines the smallest partition of S according to the labeling function L. It is defined as follows:
  $\mathsf{Part_{AP}}(S) = \{S_1, S_2, \ldots, S_n\} \Leftrightarrow S = \bigcup_{i=1}^{n} S_i : \forall i \in \{1..n\}, \forall s, s' \in S_i, L(s) = L(s') \wedge \forall s \in S_i, \forall s' \in S_j, j \neq i, L(s) \neq L(s')$

Now we are able to define the symbolic observation graph for hybrid LTL.

Definition 4 (Event-State Based SOG). *Let $\mathcal{K} = \langle \Gamma, Act, L, \rightarrow, s_0 \rangle$ be an LKS over a set of atomic propositions AP, and $Obs \subseteq Act$ be a set of observed actions of $\mathcal{K}$. The SOG associated with $\mathcal{K}$, over AP and Obs, is an LKS $\mathcal{G} = \langle A, Obs \cup \{\tau\}, L', \rightarrow', a_0 \rangle$ where:*

1. *A is a nonempty finite set of aggregates satisfying:*
   - $\forall a \in A$, $\forall t \in Obs, \forall o_i \in \mathsf{Part_{AP}}(\mathsf{Out}(a,t)), \exists a' \in A$ *s.t.* $a'.S = \mathsf{SAT_{AP}}(o_i)$
   - $\forall a \in A$, $\forall o_i \in \mathsf{Part_{AP}}(\mathsf{Out}_\tau(a)), \exists a' \in A$ *s.t.* $a'.S = \mathsf{SAT_{AP}}(o_i)$
2. $L' : A \longrightarrow 2^{AP}$ *is a labeling function s.t.* $L'(a = \langle S, d, l \rangle) = L(s)$ *for* $s \in S$*;*
3. $\rightarrow' \subseteq A \times Act \times A$ *is the action relation where:*
   - $(a, t, a') \in \rightarrow' \Leftrightarrow (t \in Obs \wedge \exists o_i \in \mathsf{Part_{AP}}(\mathsf{Out}(a,t))$ *s.t.* $\mathsf{SAT_{AP}}(o_i) = a'.S)$
   - $(a, \tau, a') \in \rightarrow' \Leftrightarrow (\exists o_i \in \mathsf{Part_{AP}}(\mathsf{Out}_\tau(a))$ *s.t.* $\mathsf{SAT_{AP}}(o_i) = a'.S)$
4. a_0 *is the initial aggregate s.t.* $a_0 = \mathsf{SAT_{AP}}(\{s_0\})$

The finite set of aggregates A of the SOG is defined in a complete manner such that the necessary aggregates are represented. The labeling function gives to any aggregate of the SOG, the same label as its states. Point 3 defines the action relation: there exists an arc, labeled with an observed action t (resp. τ), from a to a' iff a' is obtained by saturation (using $\mathsf{SAT_{AP}}$) on a set of equally labeled reached states $\mathsf{Out}(a,t)$ (resp. $\mathsf{Out}_\tau(a)$) by the firing of t (resp. any unobserved action) from states in a. Finally, point 4 characterizes the initial aggregate.

Figure 1(a) illustrates an event-state based SOG corresponding to the LKS of Fig. 1(b). This SOG consists of 4 aggregates $\{a_0, a_1, a_2, a_3\}$ and 4 edges. The initial aggregate a_0 is obtained by adding the initial state s_0 of the LKS, and any state labeled similarly to s_0 that is reachable from it by unobserved sequences of actions. Hence, a_0 contains the states s_0 and s_4. State s_2, which is reachable from s_0 by an observed action o_1, is excluded from a_0 and belongs to a_1. The same holds for s_6 which is reachable from s_4 by o_1 and belongs to the aggregate a_2. State s_3 (resp. s_7) is added to a_1 (resp. a_2) because it has the same label as s_2 (resp. s_6) and it is reachable from it by an unobserved action.

According to Definition 4, the SOG associated with an *LKS* is unique. Thus, by considering the coarsest possible partition of homogeneous successor aggregates, aggregates a_1 and a_2 in Fig. 1(b) will be merged into a unique aggregate since they have the same label. Note that SOGs can also be nondeterministic since, for instance, an aggregate can have several successors with τ (i.e. when the reached states, by τ, have different labels).

3.2 Checking Stuttering Invariant Properties on SOGs

The equivalence between checking a given stuttering invariant formula (e.g. $LTL \setminus X$ formula) on the new adapted SOG, and checking it on the original reachability graph is ensured by the preservation of maximal paths (i.e. finite paths leading to a dead state and infinite paths).

Note that a SOG preserves the observed traces of the corresponding model, thus it preserves the infinite runs involving infinitely often observed transitions. Then, the truth value of the state-based atomic propositions occurring in the formulae is visible on the SOG by labeling each aggregate with the atomic propositions labeling of (all) its states. Moreover, the d and l attributes of each aggregate allow detecting deadlocks and livelocks (unobserved cycles), respectively. The detection of the existence of dead states and cycles inside an aggregate is performed using symbolic operations (decision diagram-based operations) only.

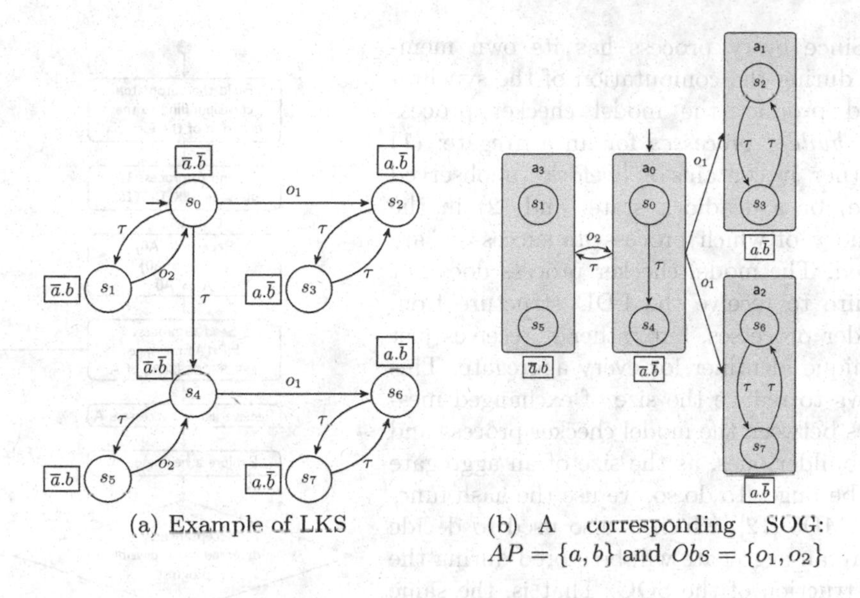

(a) Example of LKS
(b) A corresponding SOG: AP = {a, b} and Obs = {o1, o2}

Fig. 1. An LKS and its SOG

We can now establish that an *LKS* satisfies a hybrid $LTL \setminus X$ formula iff the corresponding SOG does. The reader can find the proof of Theorem 1 in [27].

Theorem 1. *Let $\mathcal{K}$ be an LKS and $\mathcal{G}$ be the corresponding SOG over Obs and AP. Let φ be a hybrid $LTL \setminus X$ formula on a subset of $Obs \cup AP$. Then $\mathcal{K} \models \varphi \Leftrightarrow \mathcal{G} \models \varphi$.*

4 Hybrid LTL Model Checker Based on the SOG

In this section, we propose an on-the-fly parallel/distributed LTL model checking approach based on the event-state based SOG. Here, our aim is to compute the synchronized product between the automaton modeling the negation of the hybrid LTL formula with the SOG (*LKS*), and check its emptiness on-the-fly.

For this purpose, a dedicated process, called *model checker process* is created (see Fig. 2). It builds the Büchi automaton of the formula negation, and then it initiates the parallel construction of the SOG simultaneously with the model checking process (i.e. computation of the synchronized product and the emptiness check). Note that this process performs model checking sequentially, while SOG construction is distributed.

Regarding the construction of the SOG, it is performed by running several processes, where each process consists of several threads. The partitioning of the building of the SOG is performed at the process level, where the load balancing between processes is performed statically by using a *hash function*. On the other hand, the partitioning of each part of the graph, for a given process, is performed at the thread level by using a *dynamic load balancing function*.

Since every process has its own memory, during the computation of the synchronized product the model checker process asks *builder processes* for an aggregate: (1) whether it contains a livelock (unobserved cycle) or a deadlock state, and (2) in the memory of which process its successors are stored. The model checker process does not require to receive the LDD structure from builder processes, but rather it receives just a unique identifier for every aggregate. This allows to reduce the size of exchanged messages between the model checker process and the builder ones, as the size of an aggregate can be huge. To do so, we use the hash function MD5 [12], which is also used to decide where an aggregate will be stored during the construction of the SOG. That is, the same function is used to statically balance the load of aggregates construction on builder processes.

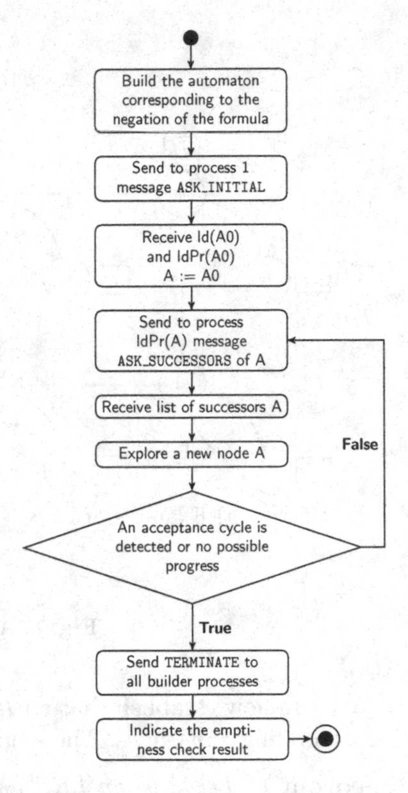

Fig. 2. Algorithm of the model checker process

In order to illustrate how the model checker process retrieves information about a SOG from builder processes, we consider the SOG sample described in Fig. 3(a). Let us assume that we have three builder processes, and that the static load balancing produces three graphs as illustrated in Fig. 3(b). In this figure, a dotted node of a graph in a process i corresponds to an aggregate such that its LDD structure is not stored by process i. Process i stores only its MD5 value (its unique identifier) and the identity of the process that should store it. For instance, in the graph built by process 1, there is only the aggregate q_a that is stored with its LDD

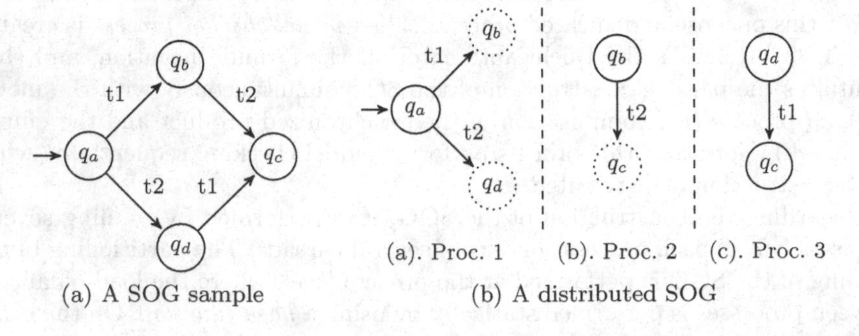

(a) A SOG sample (b) A distributed SOG

Fig. 3. Illustration of builder processes

structure by process 1. For the two other aggregates q_b and q_d, only their MD5 values are stored. Indeed, q_b is stored in the memory of process 2, while q_d and q_c are stored in the memory of process 3.

With the above in mind, we next describe the algorithm of the model checker process shown in Fig. 2. The process starts by requesting from process 1 the initial aggregate. The builder process gets as an answer its MD5 value. When the model checker asks the successors of an aggregate, it sends its request to the process storing the aggregate. For instance, for the SOG of Fig. 3(b), when the builder process wants to explore the successors of the initial aggregate, it sends a request to the builder process 1. As an answer to this request, the model checker process should get the MD5 values of aggregates q_b and q_d, and the identities of the processes storing these successors. Following the same approach, in order to get the successors of q_b, the model checker process will send its request to process 2. The termination is fully managed by the model checker process, since it may request information from builder processes even if they terminate the SOG construction. In fact, termination is achieved when the model checker process detects an acceptance run or when it is not possible to progress in the computation of the synchronization product, i.e. the result is an empty set.

Now we describe the algorithm of builder processes (see Fig. 4). The process starts by creating several threads. One of them is dedicated for communication with other processes, while the others operate in a loop as follows. At each iteration, it pops a set of markings from which it builds an aggregate. The latter is canonicalized [26] (i.e. aggregates a and a' are equals iff they have the same canonical representation), then through a hash function the thread determines if the computed aggregate should be stored by its process or to be sent to another builder process. In order to minimize communication cost, only markings of the canonicalized version of an aggregate are sent. Function `idPr(A)` returns the process identity that has to store the aggregate `A`. If an aggregate should be sent to another process, only its hash identifier is stored by the current process. Note

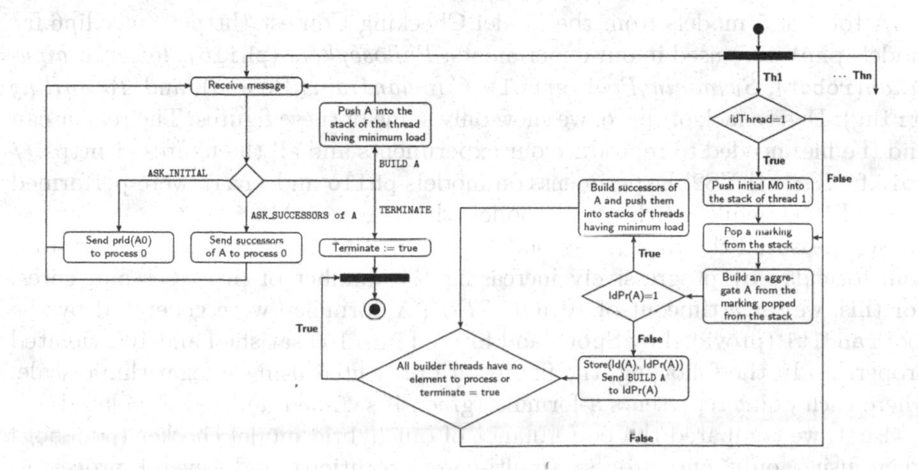

Fig. 4. Algorithm of builder processes

that only thread 1 of the first builder process has to initiate the construction of the distributed SOG by pushing an initial marking into its stack.

Different messages can be received by a builder process from the model checker process. We use the function `Receive(`*TAG, message, 0*`)` to receive a message of type TAG from process with ranking 0. Function `Send(`*TAG, message, 0*`)` allows for sending a message of type TAG to process with ranking 0. A builder process can receive the following types of messages from a model checker process:

- Message `ASK_INITIAL` corresponds to a request from the model checker process to get the MD5 value and the identity of the process storing the aggregate. This message is only received by the master builder process.
- Message `ASK_SUCCESSORS` corresponds to a request from the model checker process to get the list of successors of the aggregate having the MD5 value specified in the message. Also, information about divergence and deadlocks related to this aggregate are concerned.
- Message `TERMINATE` is sent by the model checker process in order to terminate builder processes. This message is sent when the model checker process has already performed the emptiness check.

5 Implementation and Experiments

The implementation of the hybrid model checker is based on the Spot library [13]: an object-oriented model checking C++ library that offers a set of building blocks to develop LTL model checkers based on the automata-theoretic approach.

Experiments were performed on the Magi cluster (http://magi.univ-paris13.fr/wiki/) of University Sorbonne Paris Nord and on the Grid'5000 network [8]. For the former, we used the partition `COMPUTE` which has 40 processors (two Intel Xeon E5-2650 v3 at 2.30 GHz) connected by an InfiniBand network, and 64 GB of RAM. For the latter, we used the `gros` cluster composed of 124 processors connected by a 25 Gbps Ethernet network, and 96 GB of RAM.

A total of 5 models from the Model Checking Contest (https://mcc.lip6.fr/models.php) were used in our experiments: *Philosophers* (`philo`), *RobotManipulation*(`robot`), *SwimmingPool* (`spool`), *CircularTrains* (`train`), and *TokenRing* (`tring`). Due to lack of space, we show only some of these figures. The reader can find the files needed to reproduce our experiments and all the figures at https://up13.fr/?G8tMFVS2. Experiments on models `philo` and `train` were performed on Grid'5000, while for the other models they were on Magi.

We measured the time (in seconds) consumed by the verification of 200 random formulae by progressively increasing the number of processes and cores. For this, we set a timeout of 10 min. $LTL \setminus X$ formulae were generated by the tool `randltl` (provided by Spot), and filtered into 100 satisfied and 100 violated properties. In the following, the figures are presented using a logarithmic scale, where each point represents a formula (green if satisfied and red if violated).

First, we compared the performance of our hybrid model checker (`pmc-sog`) when using only one process (multi-core execution) and several processes. Figure 5 shows the performance comparison when using 16 cores and 1, 2 and 4

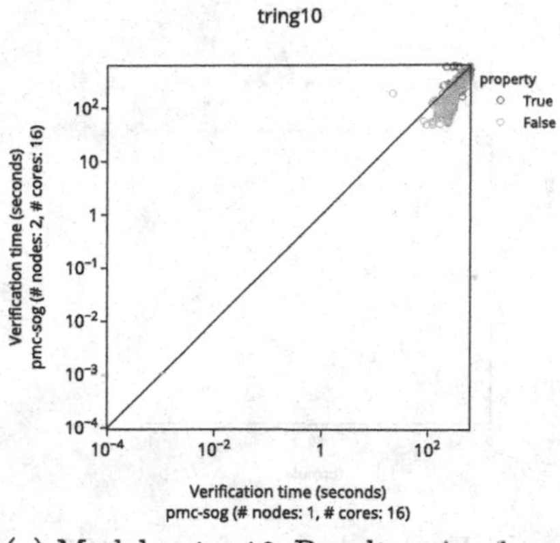

(a) Model `tring10`. Results using 1 and 2 processes with 16 threads each

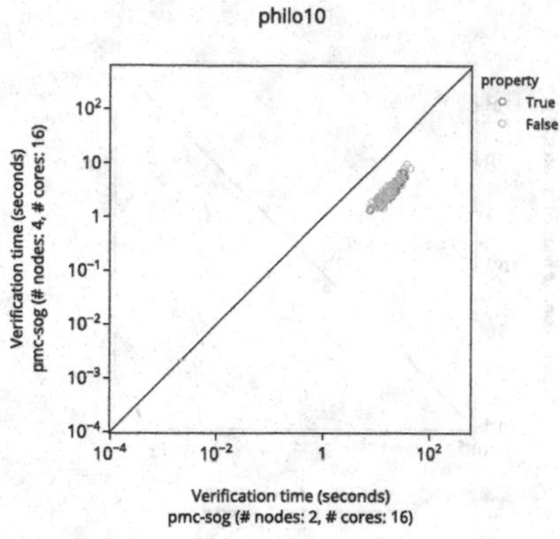

(b) Model `philo10`. Results using 2 and 4 processes with 16 threads each

Fig. 5. Comparison of performances in `pmc-sog` by increasing the number of processes

processes with models `tring10` and `philo10` as inputs. Observe that the hybrid execution outperforms the multi-core one, and the verification performance is improved by using more processes despite the induced communication overhead.

Then, we performed a comparison between our tool (`pmc-sog`) and the LTSmin model checker [22]. LTSmin (https://ltsmin.utwente.nl/) is an LTL/CTL/μ-calculus model checker that accepts inputs in different modeling formalisms, e.g. PNML, UPPAAL, DiVinE. For sake of simplicity, we choose the traditional place/transition Petri nets in PNML format, thus we run `pnml2lts-mc` in our experiments since it is the LTSmin frontend that performs LTL model checking for PNML models. We also adopted the DFS (Depth-First Search) algorithm for all approaches. It is worth noting that we only used formulae whose atomic propositions are based on states because LTSmin is a state-based model checker.

We keep all the parameters across the different model checkers the same. Tuning these parameters on a per-model basis could give faster results, however it would hide the real performance gains obtained by parallelization. We also avoid resizing of the state storage in all cases by increasing the initial hash table size enough for all benchmarked input models.

We show in Figs. 6 and 7 a selection of our experimental results. As we can observe, our approach performs better than LTSmin for big models (i.e. `robot50`, `spool5`). For instance, LTSmin could not verify 96 formulae of `robot50` due to timeout, lack of memory or unknown errors. On the other hand, `pmc-sog` could not verify 49 formulae. We also note that LTSmin has a better performance for small models (i.e. `philo10`, `train12`). Indeed, at the right of each figure the number of states explored by LTSmin during the verification of each formula, confirms this observation. For the model `robot50`, LTSmin explores 3.64×10^9 states on average for verifying violated formulae, and 2.56×10^9 states on average for verifying satisfied properties. On the other hand, for the model `train12`, LTSmin explores 4.94×10^3 states on average for verifying violated formulae,

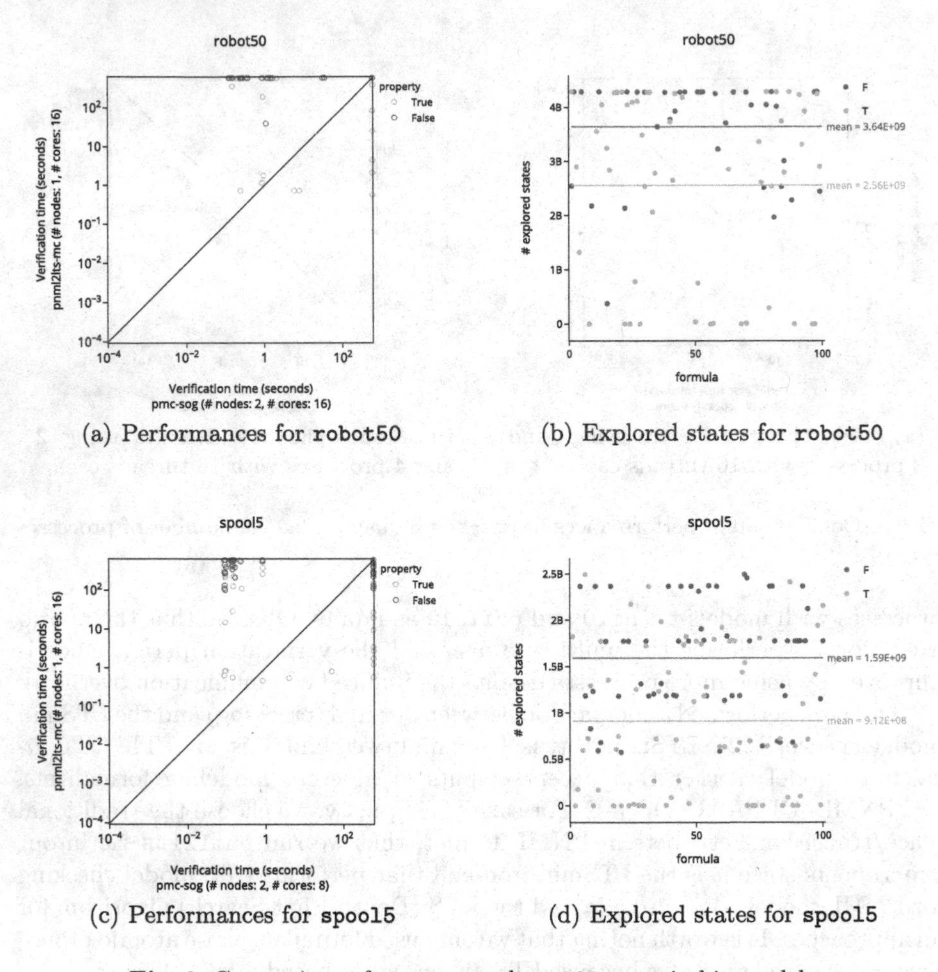

(a) Performances for **robot50**

(b) Explored states for **robot50**

(c) Performances for **spool5**

(d) Explored states for **spool5**

Fig. 6. Comparison of `pmc-sog` and `pnml2lts-mc` in big models

and 2.22×10^3 states on average for verifying satisfied properties. This disparity w.r.t. explored states allows LTSmin to quickly verify properties on small models. In this case, the performances of our tool are reduced due to the communication overhead induced by the increase of the number of processes (contrary to LTSmin that does not require any communication since it is a multi-core tool), as well as the time consumed by MD5 computation, the construction and the reduction of the SOG aggregates. Besides, our tool outperforms LTSmin for bigger models since more space memory in total is allocated by the operating system to the tool, and the storage of a SOG is split over processes. Thus, processes can be speedier as they manage less memory space to store parts of the SOG, or they can terminate the model checking while LTSmin cannot due to lack of memory.

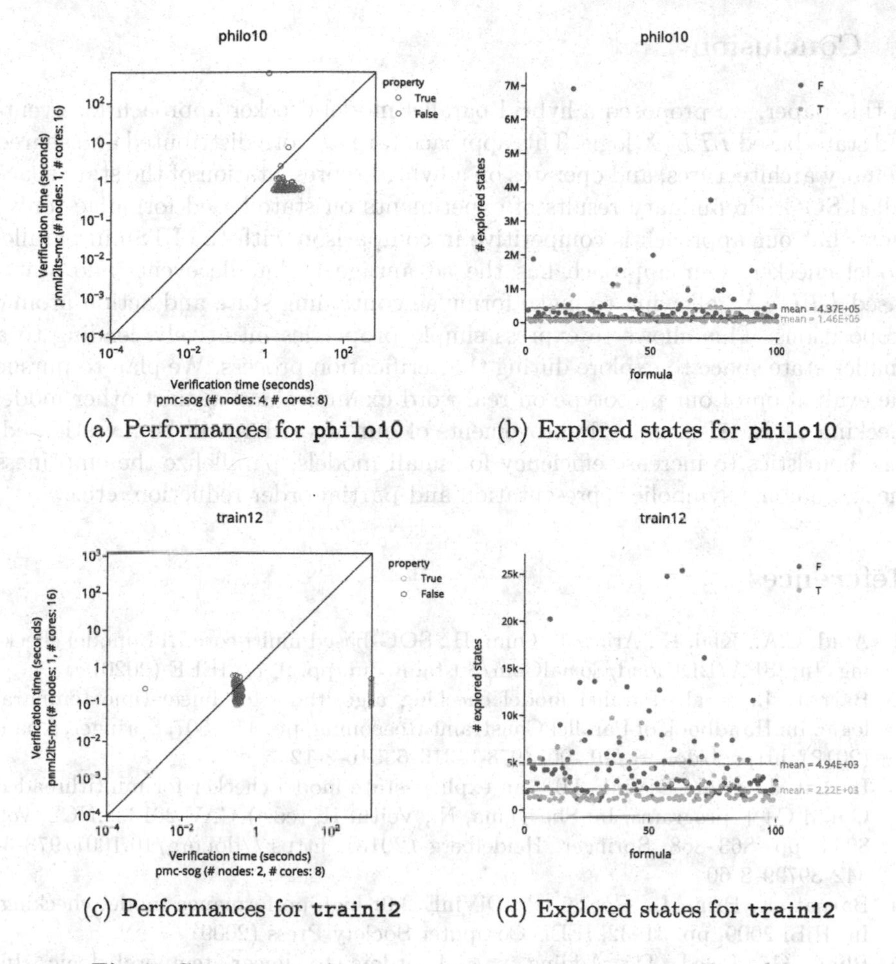

(a) Performances for **philo10** (b) Explored states for **philo10**

(c) Performances for **train12** (d) Explored states for **train12**

Fig. 7. Comparison of pmc-sog and pnml2lts-mc in small models

To improve our tool performances against relatively small models, we could use some heuristics to stop the local computation of an aggregate, and prioritize the building of the synchronized product and the search for an accepting cycle. A possible heuristic could be a predefined threshold (parameter of our tool) defining the maximum number of states per aggregate. Once this threshold is reached for a current aggregate, its construction is stopped (i.e. split the aggregate). In this case, some aggregates would be connected by a τ transition (i.e. unobserved).

As a preliminary deduction, no model checker has an absolute advantage over the other: our model checker is the fastest for checking properties that require to explore a large number of states, while LTSmin performs better for cases requiring less states to explore. Finally, it is important to emphasize that our tool is still a prototype and its results should be confirmed by more testing and improving some of its aspects.

6 Conclusion

In this paper, we proposed a hybrid parallel model-checker approach for event- and state-based $LTL\backslash X$ logic. This approach targets both distributed and shared memory architectures, and operates on a hybrid representation of the state space called SOG. Preliminary results of experiments on state-based formulae (only) show that our approach is competitive in comparison with the LTSmin parallel model checker. Our approach has the advantage to handle event- and state-based $LTL \setminus X$, allowing to make formulae containing state and action atomic propositions. This allows to express simple properties intuitively, leading to a smaller state space to explore during the verification process. We plan to pursue the evaluation of our prototype on real word examples and against other model checking tools. Also, many improvements of our algorithm will be investigated, e.g. heuristics to increase efficiency for small models, parallelize the emptiness check, combine symbolic representation and partial order reduction, etc.

References

1. Abid, C.A., Klai, K., Arias, J., Ouni, H.: SOG-based multi-core LTL model checking. In: ISPA/BDCloud/SocialCom/SustainCom, pp. 9–17. IEEE (2020)
2. Barnat, J., et al.: Parallel model checking algorithms for linear-time temporal logic. In: Handbook of Parallel Constraint Reasoning, pp. 457–507. Springer, Cham (2018). https://doi.org/10.1007/978-3-319-63516-3_12
3. Barnat, J., et al.: DiVinE 3.0 – an explicit-state model checker for multithreaded C and C++ programs. In: Sharygina, N., Veith, H. (eds.) CAV 2013. LNCS, vol. 8044, pp. 863–868. Springer, Heidelberg (2013). https://doi.org/10.1007/978-3-642-39799-8_60
4. Barnat, J., Brim, L., Rockai, P.: DiVinE 2.0: high-performance model checking. In: HiBi 2009, pp. 31–32. IEEE Computer Society Press (2009)
5. Bhat, G., Peled, D.: Adding partial orders to linear temporal logic. In: Mazurkiewicz, A., Winkowski, J. (eds.) CONCUR 1997. LNCS, vol. 1243, pp. 119–134. Springer, Heidelberg (1997). https://doi.org/10.1007/3-540-63141-0_9
6. Biere, A., Zhu, Y., Clarke, E.M.: Multiple state and single state tableaux for combining local and global nodel checking. In: Olderog, E.-R., Steffen, B. (eds.) Correct System Design. LNCS, vol. 1710, pp. 163–179. Springer, Heidelberg (1999). https://doi.org/10.1007/3-540-48092-7_8
7. Blom, S., van de Pol, J.: Symbolic reachability for process algebras with recursive data types. In: Fitzgerald, J.S., Haxthausen, A.E., Yenigun, H. (eds.) ICTAC 2008. LNCS, vol. 5160, pp. 81–95. Springer, Heidelberg (2008). https://doi.org/10.1007/978-3-540-85762-4_6
8. Bolze, R., et al.: Grid'5000: a large scale and highly reconfigurable experimental grid testbed. IJHPCA **20**(4), 481–494 (2006)
9. Bryant, R.E.: Symbolic Boolean manipulation with ordered binary-decision diagrams. ACM Comput. Surv. **24**(3), 293–318 (1992)
10. Clarke, E.M., Grumberg, O., Peled, D.A.: Model Checking. MIT Press, Cambridge (2001)

11. Courcoubetis, C., Vardi, M., Wolper, P., Yannakakis, M.: Memory efficient algorithms for the verification of temporal properties. In: Clarke, E.M., Kurshan, R.P. (eds.) CAV 1990. LNCS, vol. 531, pp. 233–242. Springer, Heidelberg (1991). https://doi.org/10.1007/BFb0023737
12. Dobbertin, H.: Cryptanalysis of MD5 compress. In: Rump Session of Eurocrypt 1996, pp. 71–82 (1996)
13. Duret-Lutz, A., et al.: Spot 2.0 — a framework for LTL and ω-automata manipulation. In: Artho, C., Legay, A., Peled, D. (eds.) ATVA 2016. LNCS, vol. 9938, pp. 122–129. Springer, Cham (2016). https://doi.org/10.1007/978-3-319-46520-3_8
14. Filippidis, I., Holzmann, G.J.: An improvement of the piggyback algorithm for parallel model checking. In: SPIN, pp. 48–57. ACM (2014)
15. Fisler, K., Fraer, R., Kamhi, G., Vardi, M.Y., Yang, Z.: Is there a best symbolic cycle-detection algorithm? In: Margaria, T., Yi, W. (eds.) TACAS 2001. LNCS, vol. 2031, pp. 420–434. Springer, Heidelberg (2001). https://doi.org/10.1007/3-540-45319-9_29
16. Geldenhuys, J., Valmari, A.: Techniques for smaller intermediary BDDs. In: Larsen, K.G., Nielsen, M. (eds.) CONCUR 2001. LNCS, vol. 2154, pp. 233–247. Springer, Heidelberg (2001). https://doi.org/10.1007/3-540-44685-0_16
17. Godefroid, P., Wolper, P.: A partial approach to model checking. In: LICS, pp. 406–415. IEEE Computer Society (1991)
18. Haddad, S., Ilié, J.-M., Klai, K.: Design and evaluation of a symbolic and abstraction-based model checker. In: Wang, F. (ed.) ATVA 2004. LNCS, vol. 3299, pp. 196–210. Springer, Heidelberg (2004). https://doi.org/10.1007/978-3-540-30476-0_19
19. Henzinger, T.A., Kupferman, O., Vardi, M.Y.: A space-efficient on-the-fly algorithm for real-time model checking. In: Montanari, U., Sassone, V. (eds.) CONCUR 1996. LNCS, vol. 1119, pp. 514–529. Springer, Heidelberg (1996). https://doi.org/10.1007/3-540-61604-7_73
20. Holzmann, G.J.: Parallelizing the spin model checker. In: Donaldson, A., Parker, D. (eds.) SPIN 2012. LNCS, vol. 7385, pp. 155–171. Springer, Heidelberg (2012). https://doi.org/10.1007/978-3-642-31759-0_12
21. Kaivola, R., Valmari, A.: The weakest compositional semantic equivalence preserving nexttime-less linear temporal logic. In: Cleaveland, W.R. (ed.) CONCUR 1992. LNCS, vol. 630, pp. 207–221. Springer, Heidelberg (1992). https://doi.org/10.1007/BFb0084793
22. Kant, G., Laarman, A., Meijer, J., van de Pol, J., Blom, S., van Dijk, T.: LTSmin: high-performance language-independent model checking. In: Baier, C., Tinelli, C. (eds.) TACAS 2015. LNCS, vol. 9035, pp. 692–707. Springer, Heidelberg (2015). https://doi.org/10.1007/978-3-662-46681-0_61
23. Klai, K., Poitrenaud, D.: MC-SOG: an LTL model checker based on symbolic observation graphs. In: van Hee, K.M., Valk, R. (eds.) PETRI NETS 2008. LNCS, vol. 5062, pp. 288–306. Springer, Heidelberg (2008). https://doi.org/10.1007/978-3-540-68746-7_20
24. Ouni, H., Klai, K., Abid, C.A., Zouari, B.: A parallel construction of the symbolic observation graph: the basis for efficient model checking of concurrent systems. In: SCSS. EPiC Series in Computing, vol. 45, pp. 107–119. EasyChair (2017)
25. Ouni, H., Klai, K., Abid, C.A., Zouari, B.: Parallel symbolic observation graph. In: ISPA/IUCC, pp. 770–777. IEEE (2017)
26. Ouni, H., Klai, K., Abid, C.A., Zouari, B.: Reducing time and/or memory consumption of the SOG construction in a parallel context. In: ISPA/IUCC/BDCloud/SocialCom/SustainCom, pp. 147–154. IEEE (2018)

27. Ouni, H., Klai, K., Abid, C.A., Zouari, B.: Towards parallel verification of concurrent systems using the symbolic observation graph. In: ACSD, pp. 23–32 (2019)
28. Sebastiani, R., Tonetta, S., Vardi, M.Y.: Symbolic systems, explicit properties: on hybrid approaches for LTL symbolic model checking. In: Etessami, K., Rajamani, S.K. (eds.) CAV 2005. LNCS, vol. 3576, pp. 350–363. Springer, Heidelberg (2005). https://doi.org/10.1007/11513988_35
29. Tao, Z., von Bochmann, G., Dssouli, R.: Verification and diagnosis of testing equivalence and reduction relation. In: ICNP, pp. 14–21. IEEE Computer Society (1995)
30. Valmari, A.: A stubborn attack on state explosion. Formal Methods Syst. Des. **1**(4), 297–322 (1992)
31. Valmari, A.: The state explosion problem. In: Reisig, W., Rozenberg, G. (eds.) ACPN 1996. LNCS, vol. 1491, pp. 429–528. Springer, Heidelberg (1998). https://doi.org/10.1007/3-540-65306-6_21

SMT-Based Unbounded Model Checking for ATL

Michał Kański[1](✉), Artur Niewiadomski[1], Magdalena Kacprzak[2], Wojciech Penczek[3], and Wojciech Nabiałek[1]

[1] Faculty of Exact and Natural Science, Siedlce University, Siedlce, Poland
{michal.kanski,artur.niewiadomski,wojciech.nabialek}@uph.edu.pl
[2] Białystok University of Technology, Białystok, Poland
m.kacprzak@pb.edu.pl
[3] Institute of Computer Science, Polish Academy of Sciences, Warsaw, Poland
penczek@ipipan.waw.pl

Abstract. A predictable and correct behaviour of nowadays more and more complex systems is one of the most important problems in Computer Science. In this paper, we deal with verification of multi-agent systems (MAS) via symbolic model checking. We represent MAS as concurrent game structures and use Alternating-Time Temporal Logic (ATL) to express properties of MAS under consideration. We provide an SMT-based implementation of unbounded model checking for ATL and preliminary, but encouraging experimental results.

1 Introduction

Nowadays, in everyday life, we rely more and more on information systems and various types of electronic devices. As the capabilities and complexity of information systems increase, the risk of making a mistake with catastrophic consequences grows. Many dangerous situations caused by software bugs have happened over the past decades. One of them was a disastrous launch of the new rocket named Ariane 5. The cause of the crash was quickly identified as a software bug in the rocket's systems. It cost approximately $370 M and delayed research into workings of magnetosphere for about four years [25].

Testing is a commonly used method of detecting errors in systems. There are various types of tests applied to detect and eliminate bugs in developed systems, e.g., unit and integration tests performed manually or parametrized and automated. Testing process greatly improves the software quality, as it helps to find bugs but it does not ensure that the system is error-free. However, such a guarantee can be provided by formal methods.

Formal methods are based on solid mathematical and logical basis. The main goal of formal methods is to provide techniques enabling the design of reliable and error-free systems. One of the formal methods is Model Checking (MC) [5, 13, 29] which is the very subject of this paper. This technique can be applied to ensure that given model of hardware or software system behaves according to

A. Nouri et al. (Eds.): VECoS 2021, LNCS 13187, pp. 43–58, 2022.
https://doi.org/10.1007/978-3-030-98850-0_4

its specification. Typically, a system is modeled as a labelled transition system, which is represented by a kind of graph. The graph nodes represent the states of the modeled system, while the edges stand for possible transitions between states. The specification is usually a set of temporal formulas expressing properties like safety (bad things never happen) or liveness (good things eventually happen). An example of the former could be: *two processes never reach a critical section simultaneously*, and of the latter: *every process reach a critical section eventually.*

One of the well known temporal logic is Linear Temporal Logic (LTL) [32] introduced by Pnueli in 1977. LTL consists of a finite set of atomic propositions, the logical conjunctives (*negation* and *alternative*), and temporal operators (X *next* and U *until*). Basing on these, additional operators can be defined, like, e.g., *conjunction*, *implication*, G *globally* (always), and F *eventually* (in the future). The LTL formulae are interpreted over *paths*, i.e., sequences of states, and hence the *linear* in the logic name.

Computation Tree Logic (CTL) [12] is another kind of temporal logic widely used in formal verification, introduced by Clarke and Emmerson in 1981. Here, the formulae are interpreted over a tree-like structure where the future is not determined, because there exist a number of possible paths that may be actually realised. This is a branching-time logic allowing to quantification over the computation paths. In CTL, every temporal operator should be preceded by A (*along all paths*) or E (*there exists a path*).

However, in the case of multi-agent systems, other temporal logics are suitable to express properties involving cooperation and strategic abilities. One of them is Alternating-time Temporal Logic (ATL) [2–4,17,18,20,22]. The strategic modalities enable to formulate properties like there exists a strategy such that a goal will be achieved by an agent, or a group of agents. Thus, ATL allows for selective quantifications over paths that are outcomes of games between (groups of) agents. For example, the ATL formula $\langle\langle A\rangle\rangle X\varphi$ means that the group of agents A has a strategy to enforce the property φ in the next step, regardless of the actions performed by the other agents.

Model checking has been used for over four decades to verify various hardware and software systems [1,8,36,37]. However, one of its biggest obstacles is a huge number of states in the verified systems, since it grows exponentially with the number of system components (e.g., agents). Usually, model checking can be reduced to a kind of a graph search problem, which could be solved using either *explicit* or *symbolic* methods. Symbolic model checking makes use of logical formulas or binary decision diagrams (BDDs) [9] to represent sets of states and transitions, and handle a number of them at once. In many cases, this approach is much more efficient than the explicit one, and symbolic representations of transition systems are often quite successful in alleviating the state explosion problem. A lot of model-checking tools exploit BDDs to represent the state spaces. These are, e.g., NuSMV [10] for verifying CTL and LTL formulae, and MCMAS [26,27] for verifying of properties expressed in CTL and ATL against systems specified in Incremental System Programming Language (ISPL) [28].

Sometimes, however, the BDDs have a tendency to an exponential blow-up in the number of variables, what impedes the verification of large systems. The methods aimed at addressing this problem include, amongst others, model checking algorithms based on propositional satisfiability (SAT) checking [35]. The paper of Biere et al. [6] is considered a breakthrough work on this topic. The authors proposed an incremental unfolding of the computation generated by the considered system up to a given step, a translation of the model checking problem to SAT, and use of satisfiability solvers [16] to search for a solution. This method, called Bounded Model Checking (BMC) [7,11,34], has been implemented by many tools, like, e.g., VerICS [19,23]. However, if the maximal bound for a given system is unknown, bounded model checking cannot, in fact, *verify* the tested property.

The Unbounded Model Checking (UMC) method, introduced by McMillan [30], addresses this problem. This approach is based on modification of Davis-Logemann-Loveland (DLL) [14] algorithm to eliminate universal quantifiers from Boolean expressions, enabling evaluation of arbitrary CTL formulas using fixed point characterizations of the CTL operators. The proposed method is extremely efficient in cases, when the resulting fixed points do not have a concise representation as a BDD, but can be succinctly described as CNF formula.

The authors of [21] show that UMC can be also applied to verification of ATL. The key issue in solving this problem consists in encoding the *next time* operator by a QBF formula and next translating it to a corresponding propositional formula. The other modal operators are computed as the greatest or least fixed points of functions defined over the basic *next time* operator.

The main contribution of this paper is a practical realization of the UMC method for multi-agent systems modeled in terms of Concurrent Game Structures (CGSs) [24], and the properties expressed as ATL formulas. We follow the theoretical results reported in [21], and provide, to our best knowledge, the first implementation of this method together with preliminary experimental results. However, we do not translate the verification problem to CNF, but we stop at the QBF level and use SMT-solver Z3 [15] to solve it. We compare the efficiency of our tool with the MCMAS model checker.

The rest of the paper is structured as follows. In the next sections we introduce CGSs, and then syntax, semantics, and recall the fixed-point characterization of ATL operators and their translation to QBF. Then, we present the most important details of implementation of our tool UMC4ATL and preliminary experimental results, followed by conclusion.

2 Concurrent Game Structures

In our approach, we model the systems under consideration by Concurrent Game Structures. The transitions between (global) states are determined by actions made by the system components. Each global transition represents a simultaneous step made by all the system components. Formally, following [21], CGS is defined as follows.

Definition 1. *A Concurrent Game Structure is a tuple* $S = <k, Q, \tau, \Pi, \pi, d, \delta>$, *where:*

- k *is a natural number defining the amount of agents. We identify the agents with numbers* $0, ..., k-1$ *so the set of agents is* $\{0, ..., k-1\}$,
- Q *is a finite set of global states, and* $\tau \in Q$ *is the initial state,*
- Π *is a finite set of atomic propositions (also called observables),*
- $\pi : Q \to 2^{\Pi}$ *is a labeling (or observation) function,*
- *moves (actions) available at a state* $q \in Q$ *to an agent* $a \in \{0, ..., k-1\}$ *are identified with numbers* $0, ..., d_a(q)$; *so given a state* q, *a move vector at* q *is a tuple* $<j_0, ..., j_{k-1}>$ *such that* $j_a \leq d_a(q)$ *for every agent* a; *then* d *is the mapping that assigns for every state* q *the set* $\{0, ..., d_0(q)\} \times ... \times \{0, ..., d_{k-1}(q)\}$ *of move vectors,*
- δ *is a transition function which assigns to each state* $q \in Q$ *and each move vector* $<j_0, ..., j_{k-1}> \in d(q)$ *a state* $\delta(q, j_0, ..., j_{k-1}) \in Q$ *that results from state* q *if every agent* $a \in \{0, ..., k-1\}$ *chooses move* j_a.

We say that a state q' is a successor of a state q if there is a move vector $<j_0, ..., j_{k-1}> \in d(q)$ such that $q' = \delta(q, j_0, ..., j_{k-1})$. Thus q' is a successor of q iff whenever the game is in state q, the agents can choose moves so that q' is a next state. A computation of S is an infinite sequence $\lambda = q_0, q_1, q_2, ...$ of states such that for all positions $i \geq 0$, the state q_{i+1} is a successor of the state q_i. We refer to a computation λ and a position $i \geq 0$, we use $\lambda[i], \lambda[0, i]$ to denote i-th state of λ and the finite prefix $q_0, q_1, ..., q_i$ of λ respectively.

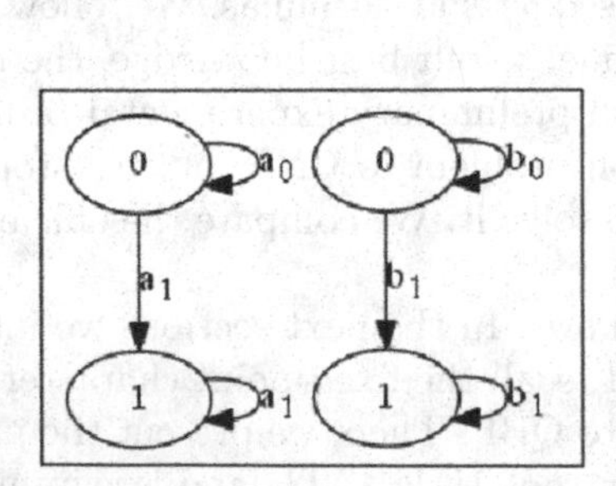

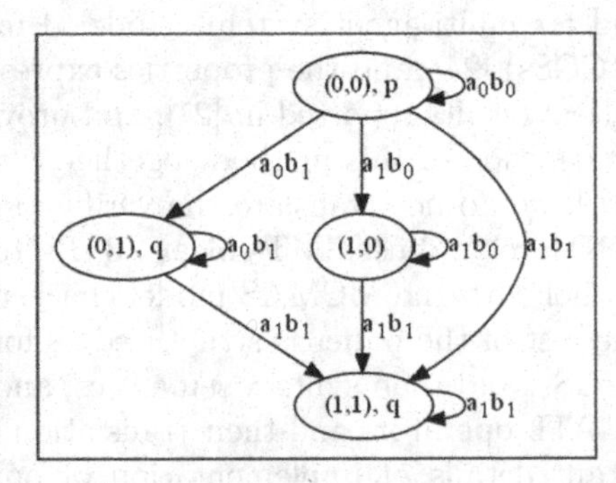

Fig. 1. An example system: two agents (left) and the corresponding CGS (right)

Example 1. In Fig. 1 (left) an example system consisting of two agents is depicted. Every agent has two (local) states 0, 1, and three transitions labeled by two actions $a0, a1$ for agent 0, and $b0, b1$ for agent 1. The CGS is shown in Fig. 1 (right). Thus, the set of global states is $Q = \{(0,0), (0,1), (1,0), (1,1)\}$. Let the initial state be $\tau = (0,0)$, and we have two propositional variables $\Pi = \{p, q\}$. Let $\pi(p) = \{(0,0)\}$, $\pi(q) = \{(0,1), (1,1)\}$, thus p is true in state $(0,0)$ and

q is true in states $(0,1)$, and $(1,1)$. The available moves and transitions are depicted as arrows. For example, $d_0((0,0)) = \{0,1\}$, $d((0,1)) = \{(0,1),(1,1)\}$, and $\delta((0,0),1,1) = (1,1)$. Note that besides numbers we additionally label actions with letters assigned to the consecutive agents.

3 Alternating-Time Temporal Logic

Before we give formal definitions, we proceed with intuitions behind ATL. A *strategy* of an agent is a plan describing what agent can do in each situation (state). Every agent can base its decisions only on the current state. A strategy for a group of agents is a tuple of individual strategies. A formula $\langle\langle A\rangle\rangle X\alpha$ means that the group A has a strategy to make α true in the next step. $\langle\langle A\rangle\rangle G\alpha$ means that the group A can cooperate in a way that α is always true. $\langle\langle A\rangle\rangle \alpha U\beta$ means that the group A can enforce β but until that happens α is true.

Definition 2 (ATL syntax). *The set of ATL formulas is defined as follows:*
- $p \in \Pi$ *is a formula,*
- *if* α, β *are formulas, then* $\neg\alpha, \alpha \vee \beta$ *are also formulas,*
- *if* $A \subseteq \{1, ..., k\}$ *is a set of agents and* α, β *are formulas, then* $\langle\langle A\rangle\rangle X\alpha$, $\langle\langle A\rangle\rangle \alpha U\beta$, *and* $\langle\langle A\rangle\rangle G\alpha$ *are also formulas.*

Additionally, the Boolean operators $\wedge, \Rightarrow, \Leftrightarrow$ are defined by the operators $\neg, \vee$. The temporal operator *eventually* is defined as $F\alpha = true\ U\alpha$. The ATL formulas are interpreted over the states of CGS. In order to define the semantics formally, we first define the notion of strategies. A strategy for an agent a is a function f_a that maps every nonempty finite state sequence $\lambda \in Q^+$ to a natural number such that if the last state of λ is q, then $f_a(\lambda) \leq d_a(q)$. Thus, the strategy f_a determines for every finite prefix λ of a computation a move $f_a(\lambda)$ for agent a. Each strategy f_a for agent a induces a set of computations that agent a can enforce. Given a state $q \in Q$, a set A of agents, and a set $F_A = \{f_a | a \in A\}$ of strategies, one for each agent in A, we define the outcomes of F_A from q to be the set $out(q, F_A)$ of q-computations that the agents in A enforce when they follow the strategies in FA; that is a computation $\lambda = q_0, q_1, q_2, ...$ is in $out(q, F_A)$ if $q_0 = q$ and for all positions $i \geq 0$, there is a move vector $h_{j_1}, ..., j_{k_i} \in d(q_i)$ such that $j_a = f_a(\lambda[0,i])$ for all agents $a \in A$, and $\delta(q_i, j_1, ..., j_k) = q_i + 1$.

Definition 3 (Interpretation of ATL). *Let* S *be a CGS,* $q \in Q$ *a state, and* α, β *formulas of ATL.* $S, q \models \alpha$ *denotes that* α *is true at the state* q *in the structure* S. S *is omitted, if it is implicitly understood. The relation* $\models$ *is defined inductively as follows:*

- $q \models p$ *iff* $p \in \pi(q)$, *for* $p \in \Pi$,
- $q \models \neg\alpha$ *iff* $q \not\models \alpha$,
- $q \models \alpha \vee \beta$ *iff* $q \models \alpha$ *or* $q \models \beta$,
- $q \models \langle\langle A\rangle\rangle X\alpha$ *iff there is a set* F_A *of strategies for each agent in* A*, such that for all computations* $\lambda \in out(q, F_A)$*, we have* $\lambda[1] \models \alpha$,

- $q \models p\ll A\gg G\alpha$ *iff there is a set* F_A *of strategies for each agent in* A*, such that for all computations* $\lambda \in out(q, F_A)$*, and all positions* $i \geq 0$, $\lambda[i] \models \alpha$,
- $q \models \ll A\gg \alpha U\beta$ *iff there is a set* F_A *of strategies for each agent in* A*, such that for each computation* $\lambda \in out(q, F_A)$*, there is a position* $i \geq 0$ *such that* $\lambda[i] \models \beta$ *and for all positions* $0 \leq j \leq i$*, we have* $\lambda[j] \models \alpha$.

Definition 4 (Validity). *An ATL formula* ϕ *is valid in* S *iff* $S, \tau \models \phi$.

Example 2. Consider the CGS of Example 1 and the formula $\phi = \ll 0,1\gg Xp$, which means that the group of agents $A = \{0, 1\}$ has a strategy that p will be true in the next step. The initial state of the system is $\tau = (0, 0)$ and there exists a transition changing state $(0, 0)$ to state $(0, 0)$. Thus, there exists a strategy for the agents to enforce p in the next step: both should perform action 0 in the initial state, so the given formula is valid, whereas the formula $\psi = \ll 0,1\gg X(p \wedge q)$ is not valid in this CGS.

4 Fixed Point Representation of ATL and QBF Encoding

In this section we briefly recall from [21] how the UMC can be used for ATL verification. The crucial point is encoding the *next* operator as a Quantified Boolean Formula (QBF). QBF is an extension of propositional logic by means of quantifiers ranging over propositions. The semantics is as follows:

- $\exists p, \alpha$ iff $\alpha(p \leftarrow true) \vee \alpha(p \leftarrow false)$,
- $\forall p, \alpha$ iff $\alpha(p \leftarrow true) \wedge \alpha(p \leftarrow false)$,

where α is a QBF formula, p is a propositional variable, and $\alpha(p \leftarrow \Psi)$ stands for a substitution of every occurrence of the variable p with Ψ in formula α.

The other modal operators are computed as the greatest or least fixed points of functions defined over the basic *next* operator. In order to obtain fixed-point characterizations of operators, we identify each ATL formula α with the set $\langle\alpha\rangle_S$ of states in S at which this formula is true that is $\{q \in Q : S, q \models \alpha\}$. If S is known from the context we omit the subscript S. Furthermore, we define functions $\ll A\gg X(Z)$ for every $A \subseteq \{0, ..., k-1\}$ as follows:

- $\ll A\gg X(Z) = \{q \in Q$: for every $a \in A$ there exists a natural number $j_a \leq d_a(q)$ such that for every state $q\prime \in Q$, every agent $b \in \{0, ..., k-1\} \setminus A$ and every natural number $j_b \leq d_b(q)$ if $q\prime = \delta(q, j_0, ..., j_{k-1})$ then $q\prime \in Z\}$.

We assume a set of agents $\{0, \ldots, k-1\}$, a set of global states Q, sets of possible actions Act_a for each agent a, and a set of protocols $P_a : Q \mapsto 2^{Act_a}$ that indicate which actions can be executed in which states. All actions are defined by means of *pre* and *post* conditions, i.e., for action c, $pre(c)$ is a set of all states from which action c can be executed and $post(c)$ is a set of all states which can be reached after the execution of action c. Furthermore, we assume that for every state q and $c_0 \in P_0(q), \ldots, c_{k-1} \in P_{k-1}(q)$ there exists exactly one state q' such that $q' \in post(c_0) \cap \cdots \cap post(c_{k-1})$. Next, we define the function δ

that assigns state $q' \in post(c_0) \cap \cdots \cap post(c_{k-1})$ to every tuple $(q, c_0, \ldots, c_{k-1})$ such that $q \in Q$ and $c_a \in P_a(q)$ for $a = 0, \ldots, k-1$. Given such a description of a system it is easy to build the corresponding concurrent game structure by taking $|P_a(q)| = d_a(q)$ and numbering actions belonging to the set $P_a(q)$ for every state q and agent a.

Next, in order to symbolically represent the (sets of) states, we assume $Q \subseteq \{0,1\}^m$, where $m = \lceil log_2(|Q|) \rceil$. Let PV be a set of fresh propositional variables such that $PV \cap \Pi = \emptyset$. Then, each state $q \in Q$ is represented by a global state variable $w = (w[0], \ldots, w[m-1])$, a vector of propositions, where $w[i] \in PV$ for each $i = 0, \ldots, m-1$. Let FPV be a set of propositional formulas over PV, and let $lit : \{0,1\} \times PV \mapsto FPV$ be a function defined as follows: $lit(0,p) = \neg p$ and $lit(1,p) = p$. Furthermore, let w be a global state variable. We define the following propositional formulas:

- $I_q(w) := \bigwedge_{i=0}^{m-1} lit(q[i], w[i])$; this formula encodes the state q over the vector w. In fact, a state is represented as a binary number.
- $pre_c(w)$ and $post_c(w)$ for every $c \in Act_1 \cup \cdots \cup Act_k$; $pre_c(w)$ is a formula which is true for valuation $q = (q[0], \ldots, q[m-1])$ of $w = (w[0], \ldots, w[m-1])$ iff $q \in pre(c)$ and $post_c(w)$ is a formula which is true for valuation q of w iff $q \in post(c)$.

Next, we translate ATL formulas into QBF formulas. Specifically, for a given ATL formula ϕ we compute a corresponding propositional formula $[\phi](w)$ which is satisfied by a valuation q of w iff $q \in \langle \phi \rangle$. In so doing we obtain a formula $[\phi](w)$ such that ϕ is valid in the structure S iff the conjunction $[\phi](w) \wedge I_\tau(w)$ is satisfiable. Operationally, we work outwards from the most nested subformulas, i.e., to compute $[O\alpha](w)$, where O is a modality, we work under the assumption of already having computed $[\alpha](w)$. The translation is as follows:

- $[p](w) := \bigvee_{q \in <p>} I_q(w)$, for $p \in \Pi$,
- $[\neg\alpha](w) := \neg[\alpha](w)$, $[\alpha \vee \beta](w) := [\alpha](w) \vee [\beta](w)$,
- let $A = \{a_1, ..., a_t\} \subseteq \{1, ..., k\}$ and let $B = \{b_1, ..., b_s\} \subseteqq \{1, ..., k\} \{a_1, ..., a_t\}$, $[\ll A \gg X\alpha](w) := \bigvee_{c_{a_1} \in Act_{a_1}, \ldots, c_{a_t} \in Act_{a_t}} (\bigwedge_{i=1}^{t} pre_{c_{b_j}}(w) \vee forall(v,$ $\bigwedge_{c_{b_1} \in Act_{b_1}, \ldots, c_{b_s} \in Act_{b_s}} (\bigwedge_{j=1}^{s} pre_{c_{b_j}} \wedge \bigwedge_{j=1}^{s} post_{c_{b_j}}(v) \wedge \bigwedge_{i=1}^{t} post_{c_{a_i}}(v) \Rightarrow$ $[\alpha](v)))$
- $[\ll A \gg G\alpha](w) := gfp_A(\alpha])(w))$,
- $[\ll A \gg \alpha U \beta](w) := lfp_A([\alpha](w), [\beta](w))$.

where gfp and lfp are based on the standard procedures computing fixed points. See [21], Sec. 6 for more details.

Example 3. Consider the CGS from Example 1 and the formula $\ll 0 \gg Xp_0$. We have, for example:

- $pre(a_0) = \{(0,0), (0,1)\}$, $pre_{a0}(w) = (\neg w[0] \wedge \neg w[1]) \vee (\neg w[0] \wedge w[1])$,
- $pre(a_1) = \{(0,0), (0,1), (1,0), (1,1)\}$, $pre_{a1}(w) = (\neg w[0] \wedge \neg w[1]) \vee (\neg w[0] \wedge w[1]) \vee (w[0] \wedge \neg w[1]) \vee (w[0] \wedge w[1])$
- $post(a_1) = \{(1,0), (1,1)\}$, $post_{a1}(w) = (w[0] \wedge \neg w[1]) \vee (w[0] \wedge w[1])$

5 Implementation

The model-checking method described above has been implemented in C# language as a tool UMC4ATL. It performs a translation of the verification problem to a QBF formula, and it uses Z3 [15] to check for its satisfiability. Z3 theory prover is a software that supports Boolean logic, arithmetic, data types, quantifiers and more.

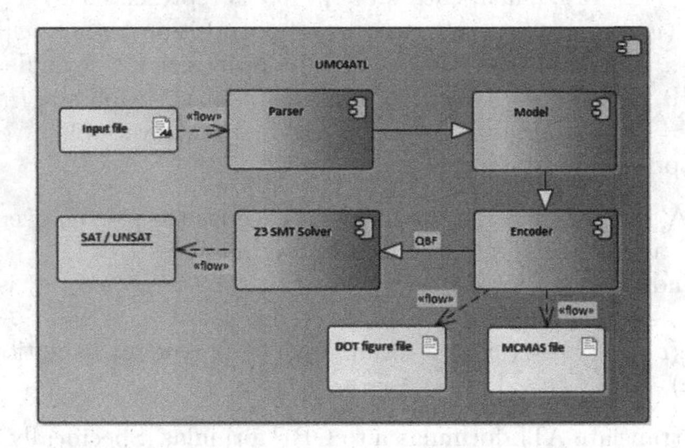

Fig. 2. UMC4ATL architecture

Figure 2 shows the overall architecture of UMC4ATL application. The very first element needed for execution of our software is an input file with agent specifications and an ATL formula to be verified. Its structure is discussed in Example 4.

The *Parser* module reads the content of the input file, checking its correctness and consistency, and then transforms it into a set of corresponding objects stored in system memory and the formula into a binary tree. Then, the *Model* module builds the graph product and computes the *pre* and *post* sets. Such prepared model objects are ready to be consumed by the *Encoder* module. In this step, if the appropriate options are set, we are translating the model into an MCMAS input file, and into DOT format to visualize the agents and CGS. Finally, we are translating the verification problem into a QBF formula to check it for satisfiability using Z3 solver. The entire tool has approximately 3200 lines of code.

Example 4. An example input file corresponding to the system introduced in Example 1 is shown below.

```
01 agent 0 2 a0,a1
02 agent 1 2 b0,b1
03 transition 0 0-a0-0
04 transition 0 0-a1-1
05 transition 0 1-a1-1
```

```
06 transition 1 0-b0-0
07 transition 1 0-b1-1
08 transition 1 1-b1-1
09 propositions 2
10 globalEvaluation 0-0
11 globalEvaluation 1-1
12 globalEvaluation 3-1
13 formula:
14 ≪0,1≫ X0
```

Each line of the input file starts with a key-word followed by parameters. Lines 1 and 2 are agent definitions, specifying the agent id, the number of local states, and the actions. Next, the lines 3–8 specify (local) transitions, and then in line 9 the number of propositions. The evaluation function is given in lines 10–12, followed by the formula at the end of file.

Besides the constructs shown in the example, we introduced also a synchronization keyword that allows to fire a global transition only if all synchronized local actions takes part in the global move. This allows for easier modeling of system specifications, such as those described in the next section.

6 Experimental Results

In this section we report our preliminary experimental results compared with the state-of-the-art BDD-based model checker MCMAS [26,27]. The experiments were performed using a PC equipped with AMD Ryzen 5 3600X CPU and 32 GB RAM running under Windows 10 OS. We used two scalable benchmarks known from literature: Train Gate Controller [33], and Castles game [31].

6.1 Experiment 1. Train Gate Controller

The Train Gate Controller scenario [33] considers a number of trains trying to access a tunnel, whose entrance is managed by a controller. The controller allows only one train in the tunnel at any time. Figure 3 shows the TGC system with two trains.

The Controller has two states, displaying a green light when the tunnel is empty, and the red light, when a train is in the tunnel. These states are marked with propositions p_0, and p_1, respectively. A train can be in one of the three states. It can be in front of the tunnel waiting for the green light, or it can be in the tunnel, or it could be away after traversing the tunnel. Due to synchronization of the appropriate actions, in Fig. 3 marked with the same labels, the Controller admits only one of the waiting trains at a time.

The meaning of propositions is as follows. p_0 means that controller displays a green light and p_1 means that controller displays a red light. Variables from p_2 to $p_{2+(3n-1)}$ mark states for each train, where n is the number of trains.

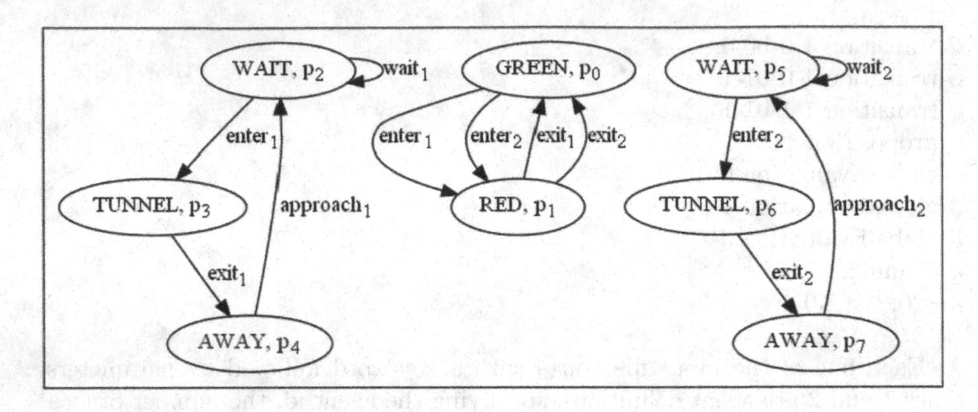

Fig. 3. Train Gate Controller system with two trains (left and right)

For example p_2 - Train1 is waiting, p_3 - Train1 is in tunnel, p_4 - Train1 lefts the tunnel. Thus, when we divide the consecutive numbers corresponding to propositions by 3, if the remainder is 2 the train is in waiting state, when the remainder is 0 the train is in tunnel, and if the remainder is 1 it means that the train lefts the tunnel.

Table 1. The ATL formulas checked against TGC specification. The column meaning from left to right: formula id, the formula, the number of nested strategic operators, the number of different coalitions in the formula, the number of subformulas, the total length of the formula.

No.	Formula	Depth	Coals.	Subf.	Length
1	$\langle\langle 0,1,2\rangle\rangle F p_0$	1	1	1	11
2	$\langle\langle 0,1,2\rangle\rangle F p_3$	1	1	1	11
3	$\langle\langle 0,1,2\rangle\rangle F(p_0 \wedge (p_3 \wedge p_6))$	1	1	1	19
4	$\langle\langle 0,1,2\rangle\rangle F(p_3 \wedge \langle\langle 0,1,2\rangle\rangle F p_6)$	2	1	2	23
1R	$\langle\langle 0,1\rangle\rangle F(p_0 \wedge (p_1 \wedge p_2))$	1	1	1	17
2R	$(\langle\langle 0\rangle\rangle X(p_0 \wedge (p_1 \wedge p_2)) \wedge \langle\langle 1\rangle\rangle X...$	1	2	2	36
3R	$\langle\langle 0,1,2\rangle\rangle X \neg p_0$	1	1	1	12
4R	$(((p_3 \vee \langle\langle 1\rangle\rangle F(1 \vee \neg\langle\langle 2\rangle\rangle G \neg\langle\langle 1\rangle\rangle F...$	5	5	10	99
1T	$\langle\langle 0,1,2\rangle\rangle X(p_0 \wedge (p_4 \wedge p_5))$	1	1	1	19
2T	$\langle\langle 0,1,2\rangle\rangle F(p_0 \wedge (p_4 \wedge p_5))$	1	1	1	19
3T	$\langle\langle 0,1,2\rangle\rangle G(p_0 \wedge (p_4 \wedge p_5))$	1	1	1	19
4T	$\langle\langle 0,1,2\rangle\rangle F(p_1 \wedge \langle\langle 1,2\rangle\rangle F(p_2 \wedge p_6))...$	3	3	3	44
5T	$((p_1 \wedge (\langle\langle 0,2\rangle\rangle F \neg p_3 \wedge p_5)) \wedge ...$	2	2	3	41

Table 1 presents formulas that have been checked against TGC specification. They are divided into three groups. The formulas 1–4 was tested in the presence of only 3 propositions. For example, Formula 2 expreses that all agents have a common strategy to ensure that eventually Train1 will be in tunnel, while Formula 4 means that for agents 0, 1, 2 there is a strategy that eventually Train1 will be in the tunnel and then a strategy that eventually Train2 will be in the tunnel. The most interesting, however, is Formula 3, which we use to test whether there may be a situation that there is a green light and both trains are in the tunnel.

The next group, the formulas 1R–4R, constitute random generated ATL formulas. Due to the lack of space, in the case of long formulas, we only show their beginning.

The third group, the formulas 1T–5T, have been tested in presence of all propositions shown in Fig. 3. For example, formula 1T expresses that there is a strategy for agents 1, 2, 3, allowing them to achieve, in one step, the state in which the first train is away, while the second train is waiting in front of tunnel. Formula 2T expresses a similar property, but does not require reaching such a state in one step, only at some time in the future. As will be shown next, Formula 2T is valid, while Formula 1T does not hold in the TGC model.

Table 2 presents the results of Experiment 1 for TGC with 2, 3, 4 and 5 trains. The column meaning is as follows. Column "No." represents the formula id, column "Sat" informs if the formula is satisfiable (Y-yes, N-no), "UMC" shows time consumed by UMC4ATL (in seconds), while the column "MCMAS" shows run-time of MCMAS.

Table 2. Results of Experiment 1, for TGC with 2–5 trains.

No.	Sat	TGC2		TGC3		TGC4		TGC5	
		UMC	MCMAS	UMC	MCMAS	UMC	MCMAS	UMC	MCMAS
1	Y	0,0174	0,013	0,0201	0,02	0,1271	0,039	0,3711	0,045
2	Y	0,0174	0,013	0,0201	0,018	0,1022	0,029	0,3704	0,045
3	N	**0,0141**	0,016	**0,0149**	0,023	**0,0167**	0,037	**0,0223**	0,035
4	Y	0,0248	0,012	0,2345	0,023	0,8891	0,030	5,154	0,043
1R	N	0,0139	0,013	**0,0146**	0,023	**0,0165**	0,034	**0,0224**	0,150
2R	N	0,0134	0,012	**0,0148**	0,020	1,3210	0,022	6,072	0,042
3R	N	**0,0122**	0,017	**0,0136**	0,024	0,0751	0,025	0,2397	0,047
4R	N	0,0130	0,013	0,0632	0,019	1,5316	0,020	5,1931	0,036
1T	N	**0,0130**	0,013	**0,0131**	0,016	0,1040	0,026	0,3512	0,036
2T	Y	0,0158	0,012	0,0188	0,018	0,1334	0,084	0,2830	0,047
3T	N	0,0181	0,012	0,0191	0,018	**0,022**	0,026	0,0670	0,043
4T	Y	0,0245	0,017	0,0255	0,023	1,3923	0,025	6,4358	0,04
5T	N	0,0301	0,012	0,0332	0,019	0,6061	0,023	2,4695	0,045

The numbers in bold show the cases where the UMC4ATL has an advantage over the MCMAS. In most cases, the performance of both tools was similar, but as the state space increased, in many cases MCMAS outperformed our tool.

6.2 Experiment 2. Castles Game

The second benchmark for testing the performance of the UMC4ATL application is a version of Castles game [31]. In this example we have two parameters: N - the number of castles, and HP - the number of hit points per each castle. Every castle has a knight, which can either defend own castle, or attack another castle. However, after every attack, the knight has to return to the castle for rest. While resting, the knight defends the castle as well.

Every attack of a single knight decreases the castle's HPs by 1, unless a knight is defending the attacked castle, what reduces the taken damage by 1. Thus, for example, if two knights attack the same undefended castle, it takes 2 HPs down. If the castle is defended, the same double attack reduces castle's HPs by 1 point. In order to keep track of the castles' hit points, we introduced another agent, called Counter. Its states correspond to the possible combinations of HPs of every castle.

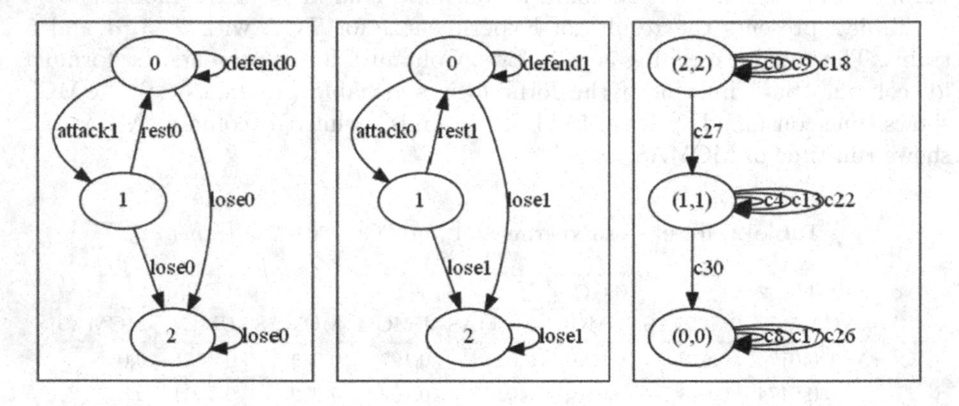

Fig. 4. Castles game with two knights (left, center), and the counter (right). Each castle has initially 2 HPs.

Figure 4 shows the system for 2 castles and 2 HPs per each. Both players start with 2 HPs, so the initial state of the system is $(0, 0, (2, 2))$. Since there is only two knights, there are only four possible outcomes of the first round of game:

- the knights defend their castles, and the state of the HPs does not change; it corresponds to the move $(defend_0, defend_1, c_0)$, and the action c_0 is synchronized with $defend_0$, and $defend_1$,
- the first knight attacks the second one which defends itself; this is the move $(attack_1, defend_1, c_9)$,
- the second knight attacks the other which defends; $(defend_0, attack_0, c_{18})$,
- both knights attack each other simultaneously and both lose one hit point. This is the only case in this setup to change the game result. It corresponds to the move $attack_1$, $attack_0$, and synchronized c_{27}.

Table 3. Results of Experiment 2. Castles game for 2 and 3 knights with 1, 2, 3 HPs

HP	N = 2		N = 3	
	UMC4ATL	MCMAS	UMC4ATL	MCMAS
1	0,036	0,031	0,146	0,025
2	0,053	0,031	1,295	0,124
3	0,063	0,048	13,951	0,254

The next rounds of the game go similarly. Of course, in the presence of more than 2 knights the game becomes much more complicated.

For this example, the formula $\langle\!\langle 0 \rangle\!\rangle G \neg lose_0$ was tested, which means that the first knight has a strategy to never lose. Table 3 shows the results of Experiment 2. The first column shows the number of hit points of every castle, while the next columns present the execution time of UMC4ATL and MCMAS (in seconds).

This benchmark shows that the UMC4ATL is not doing very well with the increase in the number of castles and their hit points, while MCMAS is more efficient here.

7 Conclusion

In this paper we presented a preliminary implementation of the Unbounded Model Checking for ATL introduced in [21]. We have translated the verification problem into a Quantified Boolean Formula and used the SMT-solver Z3 [15] to check its satisfiability. We have also compared the efficiency of our tool with the state-of-the-art MCMAS [26,27] model checker.

Our preliminary experimental results show that the UMC method works in a satisfactory way. However, we still need to introduce several optimizations and reductions - similar to those implemented in MCMAS - to increase the UMC4ATL efficiency. For example, MCMAS early prunes the unreachable fragments of the (local) state space in order to decrease the model size. Another improvement could be an on-the-fly symbolic encoding of the CGS without explicitly computing the product space. In a future work, we plan to introduce these optimizations along with checking whether the CNF translation originally proposed in [21] and the use of SAT-solvers would be more efficient than QBF solving.

Acknowledgments. The work of M. Kacprzak was supported by the Bialystok University of Technology, as part of the research grant W/WI-IIT/1/2019 of the Faculty of Computer Science and funded by Ministry of Science and Higher Education, Poland. W. Penczek acknowledges support from Luxembourg/Polish FNR/NCBiR project STV and CNRS/PAS project PARTIES.

References

1. Alur, R., Courcoubetis, C., Dill, D.: Model-checking for real-time systems. In: Proceedings Fifth Annual IEEE Symposium on Logic in Computer Science, pp. 414–425 (1990)
2. Alur, R., Henzinger, T.A., Kupferman, O.: Alternating-time temporal logic. In: Proceedings of the 38th IEEE Symposium on Foundations of Computer Science (FOCS 1997), pp. 100–109. IEEE Computer Society (1997)
3. Alur, R., Henzinger, T.A., Kupferman, O.: Alternating-time temporal logic. In: de Roever, W.-P., Langmaack, H., Pnueli, A. (eds.) COMPOS 1997. LNCS, vol. 1536, pp. 23–60. Springer, Heidelberg (1998). https://doi.org/10.1007/3-540-49213-5_2
4. Alur, R., Henzinger, T.A., Kupferman, O.: Alternating-time temporal logic. J. ACM **49**(5), 672–713 (2002)
5. Baier, C., Katoen, J.: Principles of Model Checking. MIT Press, Cambridge (2008)
6. Biere, A., Cimatti, A., Clarke, E., Zhu, Y.: Symbolic model checking without BDDs. In: Cleaveland, W.R. (ed.) TACAS 1999. LNCS, vol. 1579, pp. 193–207. Springer, Heidelberg (1999). https://doi.org/10.1007/3-540-49059-0_14
7. Biere, A., Cimatti, A., Clarke, E.M., Strichman, O., Zhu, Y.: Bounded model checking (2003)
8. Browne, M.C., Clarke, E.M., Dill, D.L., Mishra, B.: Automatic verification of sequential circuits using temporal logic. IEEE Trans. Comput. **C-35**(12), 1035–1044 (1986)
9. Bryant, R.: Graph-based algorithms for Boolean function manipulation. IEEE Trans. Comput. **C-35**(8), 677–691 (1986)
10. Cimatti, A., Clarke, E., Giunchiglia, F., Roveri, M.: NuSMV: a new symbolic model verifier. In: Halbwachs, N., Peled, D. (eds.) CAV 1999. LNCS, vol. 1633, pp. 495–499. Springer, Heidelberg (1999). https://doi.org/10.1007/3-540-48683-6_44
11. Clarke, E., Biere, A., Raimi, R., Zhu, Y.: Bounded model checking using satisfiability solving. Formal Methods Syst. Des. **19**(1), 7–34 (2001). https://doi.org/10.1023/A:1011276507260
12. Clarke, E.M., Emerson, E.A.: Design and synthesis of synchronization skeletons using branching time temporal logic. In: Kozen, D. (ed.) Logic of Programs 1981. LNCS, vol. 131, pp. 52–71. Springer, Heidelberg (1982). https://doi.org/10.1007/BFb0025774
13. Clarke, E.M., Jr., Grumberg, O., Kroening, D., Peled, D., Veith, H.: Model Checking. MIT Press, Cambridge (2018)
14. Davis, M., Logemann, G., Loveland, D.: A machine program for theorem-proving. Commun. ACM **5**(7), 394–397 (1962)
15. de Moura, L., Bjørner, N.: Z3: an efficient SMT solver. In: Ramakrishnan, C.R., Rehof, J. (eds.) TACAS 2008. LNCS, vol. 4963, pp. 337–340. Springer, Heidelberg (2008). https://doi.org/10.1007/978-3-540-78800-3_24
16. Doijade, M.M., Kulkarni, D.B.: Overview of sequential and parallel SAT solvers. In: International Conference on Information Communication and Embedded Systems (ICICES 2014), pp. 1–4 (2014)
17. Jamroga, W., Penczek, W., Dembiński, P., Mazurkiewicz, A.: Towards partial order reductions for strategic ability. In: Proceedings of the 17th International Conference on Autonomous Agents and MultiAgent Systems, AAMAS 2018, pp. 156–165 (2018)
18. Jamroga, W., Penczek, W., Sidoruk, T., Dembiński, P., Mazurkiewicz, A.: Towards partial order reductions for strategic ability. J. Artif. Intell. Res. **68**, 817–850 (2020)

19. Kacprzak, M., et al.: VerICS 2007 - a model checker for knowledge and real-time. Fundam. Inform. **85**(1–4), 313–328 (2008)
20. Kacprzak, M., Niewiadomski, A., Penczek, W.: SAT-based ATL satisfiability checking. In: Calvanese, D., Erdem, E., Thielscher, M. (eds.) Proceedings of the 17th International Conference on Principles of Knowledge Representation and Reasoning, KR 2020, pp. 539–549 (2020)
21. Kacprzak, M., Penczek, W.: Unbounded model checking for alternating-time temporal logic. In: Proceedings of the Third International Joint Conference on Autonomous Agents and Multiagent Systems, AAMAS 2004, pp. 646–653 (2004)
22. Kacprzak, M., Penczek, W.: Fully symbolic unbounded model checking for alternating-time temporal logic. Auton. Agents Multi Agent Syst. **11**(1), 69–89 (2005). https://doi.org/10.1007/s10458-005-0944-9
23. Knapik, M., Niewiadomski, A., Penczek, W., Półrola, A., Szreter, M., Zbrzezny, A.: Parametric model checking with VerICS. In: Jensen, K., Donatelli, S., Koutny, M. (eds.) Transactions on Petri Nets and Other Models of Concurrency IV. LNCS, vol. 6550, pp. 98–120. Springer, Heidelberg (2010). https://doi.org/10.1007/978-3-642-18222-8_5
24. Laroussinie, F., Markey, N., Oreiby, G.: Model-checking timed ATL for durational concurrent game structures. In: Asarin, E., Bouyer, P. (eds.) FORMATS 2006. LNCS, vol. 4202, pp. 245–259. Springer, Heidelberg (2006). https://doi.org/10.1007/11867340_18
25. Lions, J.-L., et al.: Ariane 5 flight 501 failure report by the inquiry board (1996)
26. Lomuscio, A., Qu, H., Raimondi, F.: MCMAS: a model checker for the verification of multi-agent systems. In: Bouajjani, A., Maler, O. (eds.) CAV 2009. LNCS, vol. 5643, pp. 682–688. Springer, Heidelberg (2009). https://doi.org/10.1007/978-3-642-02658-4_55
27. Lomuscio, A., Qu, H., Raimondi, F.: MCMAS: an open-source model checker for the verification of multi-agent systems. Int. J. Softw. Tools Technol. Transfer **19**(1), 9–30 (2015). https://doi.org/10.1007/s10009-015-0378-x
28. Lomuscio, A., Raimondi, F.: MCMAS: a model checker for multi-agent systems. In: Hermanns, H., Palsberg, J. (eds.) TACAS 2006. LNCS, vol. 3920, pp. 450–454. Springer, Heidelberg (2006). https://doi.org/10.1007/11691372_31
29. McMillan, K.L.: Symbolic Model Checking. Kluwer (1993)
30. McMillan, K.L.: Applying SAT methods in unbounded symbolic model checking. In: Brinksma, E., Larsen, K.G. (eds.) CAV 2002. LNCS, vol. 2404, pp. 250–264. Springer, Heidelberg (2002). https://doi.org/10.1007/3-540-45657-0_19
31. Pilecki, J., Bednarczyk, M.A., Jamroga, W.: SMC: synthesis of uniform strategies and verification of strategic ability for multi-agent systems. J. Log. Comput. **27**(7), 1871–1895 (2017)
32. Pnueli, A.: The temporal logic of programs. In: 18th Annual Symposium on Foundations of Computer Science, pp. 46–57. IEEE (1977)
33. Van der Hoek, W., Wooldridge, M.: Cooperation, knowledge, and time: alternating-time temporal epistemic logic and its applications. Stud. Log. **75**(1), 125–157 (2003). https://doi.org/10.1023/A:1026185103185
34. Vardi, M.Y.: Automata-theoretic model checking revisited. In: Cook, B., Podelski, A. (eds.) VMCAI 2007. LNCS, vol. 4349, pp. 137–150. Springer, Heidelberg (2007). https://doi.org/10.1007/978-3-540-69738-1_10
35. Vizel, Y., Weissenbacher, G., Malik, S.: Boolean satisfiability solvers and their applications in model checking. Proc. IEEE **103**(11), 2021–2035 (2015)

36. Wang, J., Wang, M., Zheng, K., Huang, X.: Model checking nRF24L01-based Internet of Things systems. In: The 9th International Conference on Information Technology in Medicine and Education (ITME), pp. 867–871 (2018)
37. Zhang, X., van Breugel, F.: Model checking randomized algorithms with Java PathFinder. In: Seventh International Conference on the Quantitative Evaluation of Systems, pp. 157–158 (2010)

Handling of Operating Modes in Contract-Based Timing Specifications

Janis Kröger[1], Björn Koopmann[2(✉)], Ingo Stierand[2], Nadra Tabassam[1], and Martin Fränzle[1]

[1] Carl von Ossietzky Universität Oldenburg, Oldenburg, Germany
{janis.kroeger,nadra.tabassam,martin.fraenzle}@uni-oldenburg.de
[2] OFFIS e.V., Oldenburg, Germany
{bjoern.koopmann,ingo.stierand}@offis.de

Abstract. The design of safety-critical systems calls for rigorous application of specification and verification methods. In this context, a comprehensive consideration of safety aspects, which inevitably include timing properties, requires explicit addressing of operating modes and their transitions in the system model as well as in the respective specifications. As a side effect, this helps to reduce verification complexity. This paper presents an extension of a framework for the specification of timing properties following the contract-based design paradigm. It provides enhancements of the underlying specification language that enable specifying mode-dependent behavior as well as how mode transitions may take place. A formal specification is given in order to enable reasoning about such specifications as well as contract operations like refinement and composition, thus enabling to make statements about mode composition. The results are discussed using a real-world example.

Keywords: Contract-based Design · Operating Modes · Timing Specifications · Mode-dependent Specifications · Mode Composition

1 Introduction

The design of safety-critical systems heavily relies on comprehensive elicitation and verification of relevant system properties. Fault tree analysis, for example, is a well-established – and in some application domains mandatory – method to investigate the impact of potential failures on the correctness of system functions and serves as an input for the development of counter-measures in the design. Similar holds for failure mode and effect analysis, which is devoted to reveal potential propagation paths of failures in the system. The development and verification of systems that are hardened against failures calls for system models that incorporate operating modes. This enables, for example, detailing the behavior of redundancy mechanisms to check whether a takeover of safety-critical functions of components in failure modes by their backups is performed

This work has been funded by the *Federal Ministry of Education and Research* (BMBF) as part of *Step-Up!CPS* (01IS18080B) and *PANORAMA* (01IS18057G).

A. Nouri et al. (Eds.): VECoS 2021, LNCS 13187, pp. 59–74, 2022.
https://doi.org/10.1007/978-3-030-98850-0_5

as expected. Modeling operating modes is also helpful for managing design complexity. For example, modern adaptive cruise control (ACC) systems in road vehicles are able to function in two modes. In *Cruise* mode, the vehicle's velocity is kept to a value set by the driver. In *Follow* mode, the ACC is controlling the velocity such that a safe distance to a previously detected vehicle in front is maintained. The active mode is selected according to the current traffic situation. The authors of [6] developed an approach in which operating modes are realized by individual components that interact via a dedicated protocol to transfer activity tokens. The approach allows to split the verification of system properties into the verification of the individual components and the correctness of the mode transition protocol, thus reducing the overall verification complexity.

Correctness of mode transitions generally concerns two entangled aspects. First, they must occur consistently as specified and do not result in unexpected behavior. In case of the ACC example, this means that at any point in time exactly one component is active. The second aspect is timing, which is closely related to the first, since mode transitions typically do not occur simultaneously among the components involved and must be coordinated. Other timing aspects may also play an important role. Safety mechanisms, for example, are specified with respect to fault tolerant time intervals, which define the maximum period of time allowed from the occurrence of a failure until the measures take effect.

Reasoning about these aspects calls for suitable specification means. Previous work [3,4] established a framework for the specification and verification of timing requirements, which employs the contract-based design paradigm [2]. Systems are modeled in terms of components. Timing requirements of the individual components are expressed in terms of Assume/Guarantee (A/G) contracts. In this work, a set of specification patterns has been defined that allows engineers to express many relevant timing aspects. However, it was already stated there that the incorporation of operating modes would be desirable. This paper aims at closing this gap. Thus, the contributions are as follows:

1. Integration of operating modes into pattern-based timing contracts, including specification of modes, transitions, and mode-dependent timing behavior
2. Investigation of mode decomposition and resulting proof obligations for common contract operations such as composition and refinement
3. Demonstration of the practical applicability based on a realistic example

The paper is structured as follows. Section 2 summarizes previous work and places our contribution in its scientific context. Section 3 introduces the basic concepts that serve as building blocks to describe system models and to reason formally about modes. In Sect. 4, we investigate general properties and identify relevant timing phenomena using a simple example system that incorporates mode-dependent behavior. Based on this, we extend relevant timing specification patterns and discuss the resulting proof obligations when applying typical contract operations in Sect. 5. In Sect. 6, the developed concepts are applied to a realistic example system to examine their practical suitability. Section 7 concludes the paper and gives an outlook on future activities.

2 Related Work

Existing research that is particularly relevant in the context of our work can be split into two areas. The first area focuses on concepts to facilitate the reusability of existing components in new environments and application contexts. The second area addresses the use of operating modes as a tool for specifying and implementing coordinated behavioral changes of systems at run-time.

Contract-based design supports component reusability by allocating responsibilities in specifications. A *contract* specifies, on the one hand, all environments in which a component is supposed to operate and, on the other hand, the expected behavior of the component if it is used in such an environment. This idea is further developed by the concept of *fine-grained contracts* [12]. Here, weak assumptions are employed for specifying alternative contexts in which components in focus can be used. Corresponding guarantees allow to specify the behavior of the components individually for each of the assumed contexts.

Reussner et al. address specifications for components that require interface changes in order to be deployed in different contexts by *parametric contracts* [10]. The concept can be used to explore different dimensions of compositionality when adapting components to new environments. Since parametric contracts are capable of modeling the dependencies between provided and required functionalities, they support predictions about the quality of service, analysis of architectural design, and automated protocol adaptation. In [11], specialized graph grammars are used to reason about these aspects. Firus et al. apply parametric contracts for measuring the performance of software components [7]. The presented method determines discrete distributions of response times while considering statistical distributions of response times of environmental services.

Cyber-physical systems are comprised of complex functions and disparate connecting components due to which the contemporary tools are not capable of providing adequate verification methodologies. The methodology proposed in [8] incorporates A/G contracts to define a small-gain theorem for the compositionality of these systems. It employs the concept of *bounded input bounded output* stability, which requires that the stability of a system is ensured if the output signal does not grow beyond all limits when the input signal is bounded.

Contract-based design has also been employed to model dynamic changes during run-time. In [6], Damm et al. exploit contract specifications to reason about the stability and safety of systems that consist of components, which provide the desired properties only in certain contexts. Control between the individual components is actively passed in terms of a particular token protocol. The method enables compositional reasoning to reduce the verification complexity.

Champion et al. have designed a mode-aware specification language called *CoCoSpec* [5], which extends the assume-guarantee paradigm and is designed to specify synchronous reactive systems. It provides benefits like rigorous feedback for fault localization, a scalable and adequate compositional analysis as well as defensive semantic analysis to identify oversights. The approach is developed as an extension of the synchronous programming language Lustre.

Kugele et al. presented an alternative solution by introducing a component model enriched with *mode-based contracts* [9], whose interface assertions are comprised of predicate logic formulas. The approach provides guidance for engineers to facilitate the use of contract-based design. It is complemented by algorithms for checking underspecification, overspecification, and specification compliance.

The present work goes along the same line as those mentioned above. It builds on top of our previous work on contract specifications [3,4] that are devoted to the timing aspect. The envisaged extension will allow the specification of component modes and, in particular, (the timing of) mode transitions, thus enables a consistent reasoning about the composition and the effects of individual modes of components or subsystems on the behavior of the overall system.

3 Basic Concepts

In the context of this work, we rely on an extended version of the system model defined in [3], which was later refined in [4]. According to this model, a system S consists of a set $\mathcal{C}$ of hierarchically nested *components*. Each component $c \in \mathcal{C}$ is equipped with three disjoint sets of *input ports* $P_i \subseteq \mathcal{P}_i$, *output ports* $P_o \subseteq \mathcal{P}_o$, and *variable ports* $P_v \subseteq \mathcal{P}_v$, which together represent the observables of the encapsulated behavioral model. In order to provide a meaningful functionality, each component must have at least one port belonging to one of these classes, i.e., $P_i \cup P_o \cup P_v \neq \emptyset$. The set of *system ports* $\mathcal{P} = \mathcal{P}_i \cup \mathcal{P}_o \cup \mathcal{P}_v$ is defined as the union of all ports of all components that are part of the system.

Based on their individual ports, the interaction of two or more components $c_1, \ldots, c_n \in \mathcal{C}$ with $n > 1$ is represented by the definition of so-called *signals* $s : \mathcal{P} \rightarrow \mathcal{P}^n$. They usually connect an output port $p_o \in \mathcal{P}_o$ with a set of input ports $P_i \subseteq \mathcal{P}_i$. For connections between two hierarchy levels, however, signals can also be defined between two or more input ports $s_{in} : p_{i_1} \mapsto (p_{i_2}, \ldots)$ as well as between two or more output ports $s_{out} : p_{o_1} \mapsto (p_{o_2}, \ldots)$ with $p_{i_1}, p_{i_2} \in \mathcal{P}_i$ and $p_{o_1}, p_{o_2} \in \mathcal{P}_o$. The set of signals of the overall system is denoted by $\mathcal{S}$.

An example system model is illustrated in Fig. 1. The system consists of two components *Function* and *Observer*, each of which has multiple input and output ports as well as a variable port called *Mode*, whose characteristics are detailed below. An interaction component *CC* serves as a converter channel, which forwards only selected events from the variable port *Function.Mode* to the *Observer.Status* event port. The ports of the components are interconnected with three signals that pass occurring events and value changes along the connections.

In order to characterize the desired system behavior, each component $c \in \mathcal{C}$ can be annotated with a set of *specifications* Φ. All elements $\varphi \in \Phi$ refer to the previously defined set of component ports $P \subseteq \mathcal{P}$ to make statements about the expected timing behavior. From a general perspective, the behavior observable at the components' interfaces could be described in terms of infinite timed traces. Though theoretically possible, it is not desirable to explicitly define the behavior in terms of trace sets over its ports. Hence, we rely on a compositional reasoning approach based on A/G contracts, which is detailed at the end of this section.

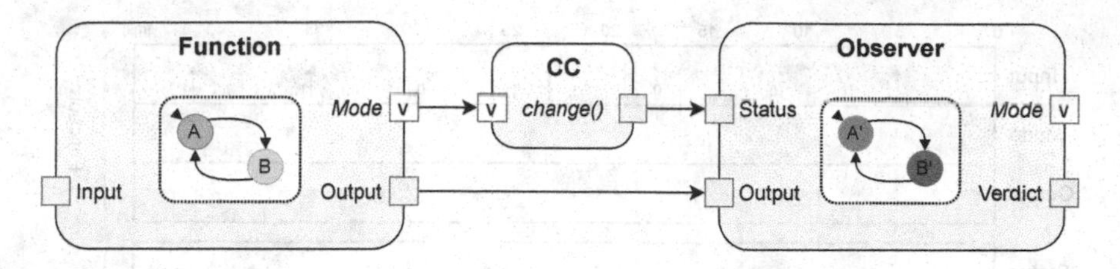

Fig. 1. Component Model of the Example System

Event Ports. The sets of input and output ports are collectively referred to as *event ports* $\mathcal{P}_{i/o} = \mathcal{P}_i \cup \mathcal{P}_o$. The behavior observable at port $p \in \mathcal{P}_{i/o}$ is restricted to its value domain Σ_p specified by the port type. We assume a special value $\perp$ to be a member of every value domain, which represents the absence of a value. A notion of *dense time* is used to characterize the occurrence of events. Therefore, we define $\mathbb{T} = \mathbb{R}_{\geq 0}$ to be the envisioned time domain. Each event port has non-absent values for all $t \in T \subset \mathbb{T}$. A single event e occurring at port $p \in \mathcal{P}_{i/o}$ is defined as a tuple $e = (\sigma, t)$ that consists of an event value $\sigma \in \Sigma_p$ and a time of occurrence $t \in T$. This allows us to describe the semantics of event ports in terms of timed traces, for which we use definitions from [4].

A *timed trace* over p is defined as an infinite sequence $\omega_p = (\sigma_i, t_i)_{i \in \mathbb{N}}$, in which $\sigma_i \in \Sigma_p$ are elements from the value domain and $(t_i)_{i \in \mathbb{N}}$ forms a monotonic sequence of time instances. We require all timed traces to be non-zeno, i.e., for each $t \in \mathbb{T}$ exists (σ_i, t_i) such that $t_i \geq t$. Moreover, we denote the set of timed traces observable at port p by $\Omega_p = \{\omega = (\sigma_i, t_i)_{i \in \mathbb{N}}\}$. For each port set P, we define a set of timed traces $(\boldsymbol{\sigma}_i, t_i)_{i \in \mathbb{N}}$ over P, where $\boldsymbol{\sigma}_i = (\sigma_1, \ldots, \sigma_n) \in \Sigma_{p_1} \times \cdots \times \Sigma_{p_n}$ holds. Similar to the consideration of individual ports, we denote $\Omega_P = \{\omega_P = (\boldsymbol{\sigma}_i, t_i)_{i \in \mathbb{N}}\}$. Based on this, the set of *possible timed traces* observable at the component interfaces can be characterized by a timed language $L_P = \Omega_P$.

Variable Ports. In order to reason about the evolution of discrete variables over time, we extend the original system model to include *variable ports* $\mathcal{P}_v$. Just like event ports, each variable port has a clearly defined value domain V_p. In contrast to event ports, variable ports have a specified value at each point in time $t \in \mathbb{T}$, which evolves at discrete time points, i.e., no absent values exist. The behavior of a variable port $p \in \mathcal{P}_v$ can thus be characterized as a *value history* $v_p : \mathbb{T} \rightarrow V_p$ that maps a well-defined value to each time point $t \in \mathbb{T}$.

To enable the interaction between ports of the two classes, we introduce two new event types, namely *set()* and *change()*, that occur on an implicitly defined, *virtual* event port $p_{i/o}(p) \in \mathcal{P}_{i/o}$ that is assigned to each variable port p:

1. *set(p, v)* events represent the assignment of a new value $v \in V_p$ to $p \in \mathcal{P}_v$ and can be called to initiate value changes. Assuming a *set()* event occurring at time $t_i \in \mathbb{T}$, the value of p is updated to $v_p(t_{i+1}) = v$ at $t_{i+1} \in \mathbb{T}$.
2. *change(p, v)* events indicate a change in the value of $p \in \mathcal{P}_v$ and can be used to react to value changes. Whenever a time point $t_i \in \mathbb{T}$ exists such that $v_p(t_i) \neq v_p(t_{i-1}) \wedge v_p(t_i) = v$, a *change()* event occurs at time t_i.

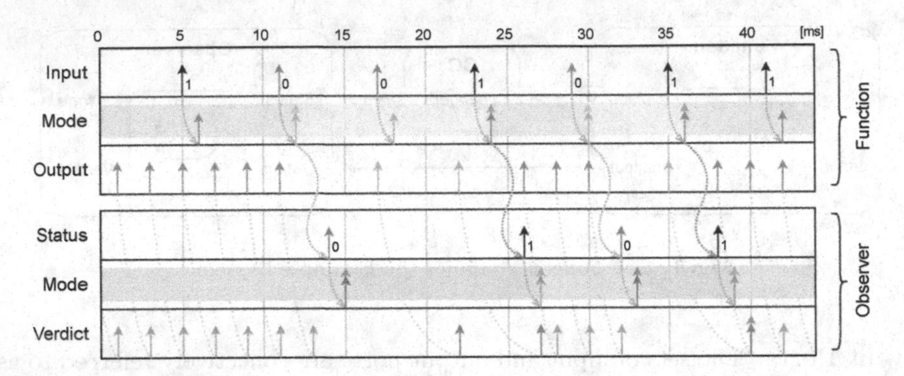

Fig. 2. Interaction Between Event and Variable Ports

For both events, the explicit specification of $v \in V_p$ is optional. In case of a *set()* event, omitting v means that an arbitrary value from V_p is set to p. Omitting v in a *change()* event allows any change of the value of p. Since we will later need to reason about traces of *change()* events, we finally define a *change event trace* $(change()_i, t_i)_{i \in \mathbb{N}}$ for each $p_{i/o}(p)$ that contains all *change(p)* events.

Specifications. Components can be equipped with *specifications* $\varphi \in \Phi$, each consisting of an A/G contract $\mathscr{C}$. It induces a set of infinite timed traces that conform to the specified properties and thus characterize valid system behavior. All specifications are defined over the components' interfaces, i.e., event and variable ports $P_\varphi \subseteq P$. To keep things simple, we assume exactly one contract $\mathscr{C}_c$ to be assigned to each component $c \in \mathcal{C}$ that defines a specification φ_c. The set of *valid timed traces* of c with respect to φ_c is denoted by L_φ. We say, c *satisfies* φ_c, written $c \models \varphi_c$, if $L_P \subseteq L_\varphi$. Finally, we define $S \models \Phi \iff \forall c \in \mathcal{C} : c \models \varphi_c$.

4 Operating Modes

In general, an *operating mode* is defined as a predicate over a set of observables, i.e., event and variable ports that are part of or accessible by a component in focus. We assume each $c \in \mathcal{C}$ to implicitly possess a dedicated variable port $p_m \in P_v$ called *Mode*, which has a *mode history* $m_c(t) = v_{p_m}(t)$ with $t \in \mathbb{T}$. The *active mode* $m_c(t)$ of c directly results from the initial mode $m_c(0) \in V_{p_m}$ as well as the sequence of *set()* events over $p_{i/o}(p_m)$ that have occurred up to the current time t. The set of modes M_c of a component is given by $M_c = V_{p_m}$, where V_{p_m} has either been explicitly defined or is implicitly derived from the set of values referenced by the set of specifications Φ. The change event trace $(change()_i, t_i)_{i \in \mathbb{N}}$ of port $p_{i/o}(p_m)$ is abbreviated as $(m_i, t_i)_{i \in \mathbb{N}}$. For traces $(m_i, t_i)_{i \in \mathbb{N}}$, we define a *time-bounded mode-set projection* $(m_i, t_i)_{M,I} = \{(m_i, t_i) \mid m_i \in M \land t_i \in I\}$, where M is a set of modes and I is either a left-closed, right-open time interval $I = [a, b)$ or an open time interval $I = (a, b)$ with $a, b \in \mathbb{T}$ and $a < b$.

To shed some light on the interaction of events occurring at the components' interfaces and the evolution of their modes, we again consider the example system presented in Sect. 3. Figure 2 depicts a set of corresponding example traces. The *Function* and *Observer* components sequentially process a sequence of events. The first of the two receives periodic *Input* events that occur every 6 ms. Depending on the value of the *Input* event, which is either 0 or 1, the variable port *Function.Mode* is set with a delay of 1 ms. The effects of the *set(Function.Mode, A)* and *set(Function.Mode, B)* events on the *Mode* port of the *Function* component can be seen in the lines below the *Mode* line. Some of them lead to changes in the mode value and thus to the occurrence of *change()* events at the virtual event port $p_{i/o}(p_{m_F})$. They are forwarded to the *Status* port of the *Observer* via the converter channel *CC*, which filters out events other than *change()* events. Additionally, the *Function* component adapts the frequency of the emitted *Output* events according to its active mode $m_F(t)$, i.e., by using a period length of 2 ms in mode A and a period length of 5 ms in mode B.

The *Observer* component receives the *Output* events and evaluates whether the observed behavior is consistent with the (time-delayed) knowledge about the mode of the functional component. To this end, it stores received mode changes in $m_O(t)$. It creates *Verdict* events to publish the result of the evaluation. A mode-dependent time span of 2 ms in mode A' and 5 ms in mode B' is required to create the verdict. Although a detailed description of the evaluation mechanism is omitted here, the example traces in Fig. 2 highlight the causal relations between events and the propagation of mode changes through the system.

The example illustrates the importance of a consistent use of evaluation times at which predefined mode conditions are evaluated to check whether a given mode-dependent behavior is valid or required in order to fulfill the specification. In the context of this work, we rely on simple *evaluation time points* that are fully synchronized with the occurrence of events. Moreover, we distinguish two classes of specification parts that are used to formulate any $\varphi \in \Phi$:

- *Generative* parts specify the occurrence of events according to a specific model, such as the periodic *Output* events generated by the *Function* component. The validity of a mode condition $\exists m \in M_{cond} : m_c(t_{eval}) = m$ is evaluated at the (anticipated) time of occurrence $t_{eval} = t_e^{\uparrow} \in \mathbb{T}$ of the event $e \in \Sigma_p$ to be generated at port $p \in P_{i/o}$ of a component $c \in \mathcal{C}$.
- *Reactive* parts specify the reaction of a component to instances of trigger events $e \in \Sigma_p$, as for example the *Verdict* events that occur as a result of the *Output* events. In this case, a mode condition $\exists m \in M_{cond} : m_c(t_{eval}) = m$ is evaluated at time $t_{eval} = t_e^{\uparrow} \in \mathbb{T}$ of the event e to be reacted to.

A missing puzzle piece is a tool to reason about the relationships between modes at different hierarchy levels, which are required to formulate consistent specifications and to perform, for example, virtual integration tests. For this purpose, we require the modes M_c of a component $c \in \mathcal{C}$ to be explicitly mapped to the modes of the lower-level components. In this context, a well-defined *mode mapping function* $\mu : M_{c'} \rightarrow M_c$ between the lower-level modes $M_{c'} = M_{sub_1} \times \cdots \times M_{sub_n}$ with $n \in \mathbb{N}_0$ and the top-level modes M_c must exist. As a result, two obligatory design tasks for the decomposition of components are derived:

1. Specify the individual modes of all lower-level components.
2. Define a mapping μ between top-level mode M_c and lower-level modes $M_{c'}$.

By applying this approach during each component decomposition, a tree-like hierarchy between modes is established, in which well-defined and traceable relationships between modes at different hierarchy levels exist. Note that the mode-dependent behavior of all lower-level components must refine the behavior of the decomposed component on the next higher hierarchy level.

5 Specification Patterns

To facilitate the specification of modes and mode-dependent behavior, we will extend two well-established timing specification patterns that allow to specify repetitive event occurrences and latencies. The basic idea is to enhance each pattern with an optional mode condition that specifies a set of modes M in which it has to be fulfilled. Since we assume a use in contract-based design, we will define consistent extensions for use in assumptions and guarantees.

On the assumption side, we will allow mode-dependent counterparts of general assumptions. This enables the formulation of more precise and situation-tailored constraints on the component's context. An even more significant reason for introducing mode-dependent assumptions is the advantage in terms of analyzability, since undefined or inconsistent mode combinations can be detected more easily. On the guarantee side, we need to define which mode is valid initially, which mode transitions exist, when and in what period these may be taken, and how the mode-dependent timing behavior of the component in focus looks like. In addition, immediate effects of mode changes in terms of adaptions in internal or output behavior will be described with mode-dependent guarantees.

In both cases, we may need to consider the behavior *before* or *after* a mode change takes effect in order to obtain a consistent and well-defined set of specifications. Inconsistencies could arise, for example, when leaving a specific mode and switching to another mode, in which a required input behavior is not (yet) provided by the interacting components. Two conceivable solutions to this problem would be to either ensure the provision of corresponding input events before the mode change is implemented or to define a limited period of time in which the absence of the required input signal is tolerated after completing the transition.

In this context, we introduce *pre-* and *post-phases* that enable to permit temporary deviations from mode-dependent behavior within a predefined time interval. Pre-phases, on the one hand, specify a kind of "settling phase" from the time of a mode change $t_b \in \mathbb{T}$ to a fixed time bound $t_b + D_{pre}$ with $D_{pre} \in \mathbb{T}$, in which both the specified behavior of the active mode and (parts of) the behavior of the previous mode may apply. Post-phases, on the other hand, define a "tail phase" that starts with another mode change at time $t_d \in \mathbb{T}$ and ends

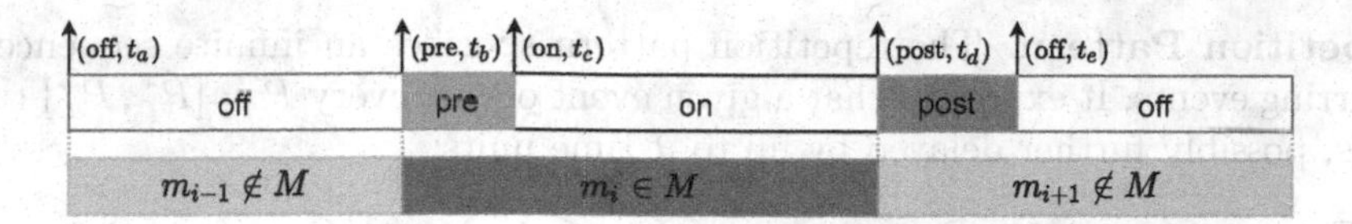

Fig. 3. Specification Pattern States and Component Modes

at $t_d + D_{post}$ with $D_{post} \in \mathbb{T}$ at the latest. Within this period, the specifications of the active mode as well as the specifications of the previous mode pose valid behavior. In the following, we assume default durations $D_{pre} = 0$ as well as $D_{post} = 0$ for generative and $D_{post} = \infty$ for reactive specifications, respectively.

The resulting sequence of specification pattern states is illustrated in Fig. 3. For $(m_i, t_i)_{i \in \mathbb{N}}$, we inductively define *specification state traces* $(state_i, t_i)_{i \in \mathbb{N}}$ with $state_i \in \{\text{pre}, \text{on}, \text{post}, \text{off}\}$. The initial state of each trace is set to

$$(state_0, t_0) = \begin{cases} (\text{on}, 0) & \text{if } m_c(0) \in M \\ (\text{off}, 0) & \text{if } m_c(0) \notin M \end{cases} \tag{1}$$

based on the initial mode $m_c(0) \in M$ of the component in focus. For $(state_i, t_i)$ and $(m_j, t_j)(m_{j+1}, t_{j+1}) \cdots = (m_i, t_i)_{(t_i, \infty)}$, we extend all traces by

1. If $state_i = \text{off}$:

$$(state_{i+1}, t_{i+1}) = \begin{cases} (\text{off}, t_j) & \text{if } m_j \notin M \\ (\text{pre}, t_j) & \text{if } m_j \in M \end{cases} \tag{2}$$

$$(state_{i+2}, t_{i+2}) = (\text{on}, t_{i+2}) \wedge t_{i+2} \in T_{pre} \quad \text{if } m_j \in M \tag{3}$$

2. If $state_i = \text{on}$:

$$(state_{i+1}, t_{i+1}) = \begin{cases} (\text{on}, t_j) & \text{if } m_j \in M \\ (\text{post}, t_j) & \text{if } m_j \notin M \end{cases} \tag{4}$$

$$(state_{i+2}, t_{i+2}) = (\text{off}, t_{i+2}) \wedge t_{i+2} \in T_{post} \quad \text{if } m_j \notin M \tag{5}$$

with $T_{pre} = [t_j, \min(t_j + D_{pre}, t_k | (m_k, t_k)_{M_c \setminus M, [t_{j+1}, \infty)}))$ and $T_{post} = [t_j, \min(t_j + D_{post}, t_k \mid (m_k, t_k)_{M, [t_{j+1}, \infty)}))$. In order to evaluate $st = (state_i, t_i)_{i \in \mathbb{N}}$ at time t, we define a *specification state function* $S_{st} : \mathbb{T} \to \{\text{pre}, \text{on}, \text{post}, \text{off}\}$ with

$$S_{st}(t) = \begin{cases} s_0 & \text{if } \exists (s_1, t_1) \in (state_i, t_i)_{i \in \mathbb{N}} : t < t_1 \\ s_i & \text{if } \exists (s_i, t_i)(s_{i+1}, t_{i+1}) \in (state_i, t_i)_{i \in \mathbb{N}} : t_i \leq t < t_{i+1} \end{cases} \tag{6}$$

that returns the active specification state. The *specification state projection* $\text{pr}_{st, \mathscr{S}}((\sigma_i, t_i)_{i \in \mathbb{N}}) = \{(\sigma_i, t_i) \mid S_{st}(t_i) \in \mathscr{S}\}$ extracts all events from $(\sigma_i, t_i)_{i \in \mathbb{N}}$ that occur during the validity of one of the states $\mathscr{S}$. Note that potentially infinitely many traces $(state_i, t_i)_{i \in \mathbb{N}}$ exist for every $(m_i, t_i)_{i \in \mathbb{N}}$. Finally, we define $St : (\Sigma \times \mathbb{T})^\omega \to 2^{(\Sigma \times \mathbb{T})^\omega}$, which returns all state traces for a given change event trace. Since each pattern is assigned to exactly one component that has a single mode port by definition, explicitly specifying $(m_i, t_i)_{i \in \mathbb{N}}$ is optional.

Repetition Pattern. The repetition pattern specifies an infinite sequence of recurring events. It expresses that a given event occurs every $P = [P^-, P^+]$ time units, possibly further delayed by up to J time units:

Event `occurs every` P `with jitter` J `in mode` M `pre` D_{pre} `post` D_{post} .

In order to keep things simple, we require $J < P^-$. The pattern is a member of the class of *generative* specifications and can thus be used either in assumptions or guarantees. Its mode-independent semantics is defined by a family of languages $L_{rep}(e, P^-, P^+, J)$, where e represents the *Event*:

$$L_{rep} = \{(e, t_i)_{i\in\mathbb{N}} \mid t_i = u_i + j_i \wedge u_0 \in [0, P^+] \wedge u_{i+1} - u_i \in P \wedge j_i \in [0, J]\} \quad (7)$$

The syntax extensions adding support for handling operating modes are highlighted with an underline. Based on the definitions from the previous sections, the semantics of the mode-dependent repetition pattern is defined as

$$\begin{aligned} L^M_{rep} = \{\mathrm{pr}_{st,\{\mathrm{on},\mathrm{post}\}}((e, t_i)_{i\in\mathbb{N}}) \mid \exists st \in St \wedge t_i = u_i + j_i \wedge \\ u_0 \in [t_{init}, t_{init} + P^+] \wedge u_{i+1} - u_i \in U \wedge j_i \in [0, J]\} \end{aligned} \quad (8)$$

such that $\exists(\mathrm{on}, t_{init}) \in st : \nexists(\mathrm{on}, t') \in st \wedge t' < t_{init}$ and

$$U = \begin{cases} P & \text{if } \nexists(\mathrm{on}, t_{on}) \in st : u_i < t_{on} \leq u_{i+1} \\ t_{on} - u_i + [0, P^+] & \text{if } \exists(\mathrm{on}, t_{on}) \in st : u_i < t_{on} \leq u_{i+1} \end{cases} . \quad (9)$$

Reaction Pattern. The reaction pattern expresses a "classical" latency between two causally related events. It specifies that an f event occurs $I = [I^-, I^+]$ after each occurrence of a related trigger event e:

`Reaction(`*Event*`,`*Event*`) within` I `in mode` M `pre` D_{pre} `post` D_{post} .

The pattern belongs to the class of *reactive* specifications and can thus only be used in guarantees. Its original semantics is defined by $L_{rea}(e, f, I^-, I^+)$:

$$L_{rea} = \{(\sigma_i, t_i)_{i\in\mathbb{N}} \mid \forall(e, t_i)\exists(f, t_j) : t_j - t_i \in I\} \quad (10)$$

Again, the required syntax extensions to specify M, D_{pre}, and D_{post} are indicated with an underline. The mode-dependent reaction pattern specifies a reaction to each trigger event e that occurs while a mode $m \in M$ is active, which only becomes visible within the validity period and the subsequent post-phase:

$$\begin{aligned} L^M_{rea} = \{(\sigma_i, t_i)_{i\in\mathbb{N}} \mid \exists st \in St \wedge \forall(e, t_i) \in \mathrm{pr}_{st,\{\mathrm{on}\}}((e, t_i)_{i\in\mathbb{N}}) : \\ \exists(f, t_j) \in (f, t_j)_{j\in\mathbb{N}} : t_j - t_i \in I \vee \exists(\mathrm{off}, t_j) \in st : t_i < t_j \wedge t_j - t_i \in I\} \end{aligned} \quad (11)$$

The use of the concepts requires a thorough consideration of resulting proof obligations. When composing components with mode-based specifications, ensuring consistency is of key importance. This must be ensured for both mode-dependent behavior and mode transitions including their pre- and post-phases

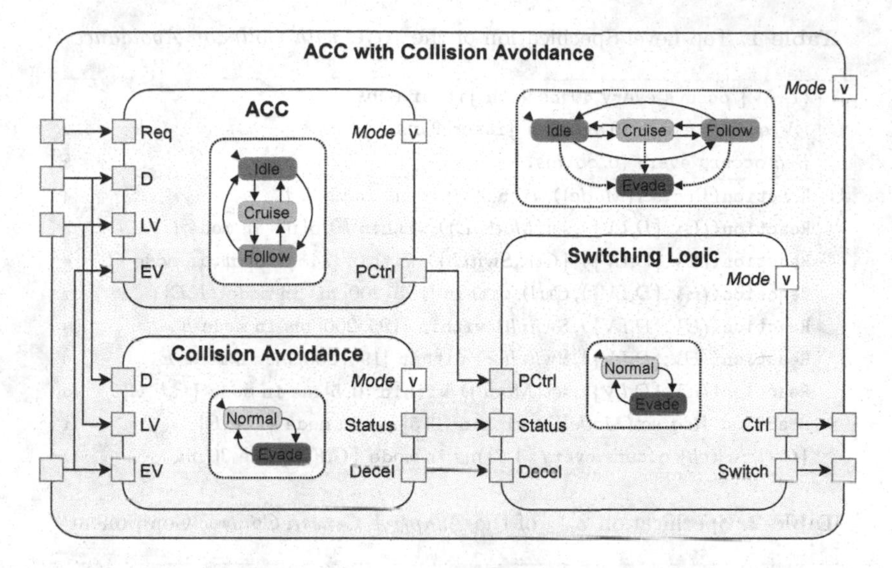

Fig. 4. Component Model of the *ACC with Collision Avoidance*

to enable error-free interaction, i.e., to show that mode changes do not lead to inconsistent states. In addition, lower-level modes must refine their associated higher-level modes. As a consequence, it is required to prove that the behavior in all operating modes is correct with respect to the assumed environments and that valid transitions are taken when the environment changes.

6 Application Example

To illustrate the approach for handling operating modes, we consider an *Adaptive Cruise Control with Collision Avoidance* (ACCwCA) as described in [1]. The *ACCwCA* is an advanced driver assistance system that possesses a number of modes, namely *Idle* (I), *Cruise* (C), *Follow* (F), and *Evade* (E). Initially, the system is in *Idle* mode. After activation, it maintains a constant speed set by the driver in *Cruise* mode. If a slower vehicle is ahead of the ego vehicle, the *ACCwCA* adapts the speed to the leading vehicle and maintains a safe minimum distance in *Follow* mode. Additionally, it provides a collision avoidance functionality to perform emergency braking maneuvers in *Evade* mode if the distance between the leading and the ego vehicle falls below a safety-critical threshold. A component model of the system in focus is depicted in Fig. 4.

The top-level specification of the *ACCwCA* is shown in Table 1. An upstream sensor processing periodically provides the distance D to the vehicle ahead and the velocity LV of the leading vehicle (line 1). The ego velocity EV is received from another external system (line 2). If activated, the *ACCwCA* computes regular updates of the control values *Ctrl* as well as *Switch* values that indicate how the values are to be interpreted. With the occurrence of a *Req* event in mode

Table 1. Top-Level Specification of the *ACC with Collision Avoidance*

A	{*D,LV*} `occurs every` 40 *ms* `with jitter` 5 *ms*.	1
	EV `occurs every` 10 *ms* `with jitter` 2 *ms*.	2
	Req `occurs every` $(0, \infty)$ *ms*.	3
G	`Reaction(`*Req*`,`set(*Mode*)`)` `within` $(0, 5]$ *ms* `in mode` *I*.	4
	`Reaction((`*EV*,{*D,LV*}`),`set(*Mode,E*)`)` `within` $(0, 5]$ ms `in mode` *I*.	5
	`Reaction((`*EV*,{*D,LV*}`),`{*Ctrl,Switch*}`)` `within` $[245, 250]$ *ms* `in mode` *C*.	6
	`Reaction((`*EV*,{*D,LV*}`),`*Ctrl*`)` `within` $[195, 200]$ *ms* `in mode` {*F,E*}.	7
	`Reaction((`*EV*,{*D,LV*}`),`*Switch*`)` `within` $[195, 200]$ *ms* `in mode` *F*.	8
	`Reaction((`*EV*,{*D,LV*}`),`*Switch.2*`)` `within` $[195, 200]$ *ms* `in mode` *E*.	9
	`Reaction((`*EV*,{*D,LV*}`),`set(*Mode*)`)` `within` $(0, 5]$ ms `in mode` {*C,F,E*}.	10
	`Reaction(`*Req*`,`set(*Mode,I*)`)` `within` $(0, 5]$ *ms* `in mode` {*C,F,E*}.	11
	{*Ctrl,Switch*} `occurs every` $[3, 7]$ *ms* `in mode` {*C,F,E*} `pre` 30 *ms*.	12

Table 2. Specification $\mathscr{C}_{acc}$ of the *Adaptive Cruise Control* Component

A	{*D,LV*} `occurs every` 40 *ms* `with jitter` 5 *ms* `in mode` {*C,F*}.	1
	EV `occurs every` 10 *ms* `with jitter` 2 *ms* `in mode` {*C,F*}.	2
	Req `occurs every` $(0, \infty)$ *ms*.	3
G	`Reaction(`*Req*`,`set(*Mode,*{*C,F*})`)` `within` $(0, 1]$ *ms* `in mode` *I*.	4
	`Reaction(`*Req*`,`set(*Mode,I*)`)` `within` $(0, 1]$ *ms* `in mode` {*C,F*}.	5
	`Reaction((`*EV*,{*D,LV*}`),`set(*Mode*)`)` `within` $(0, 1]$ *ms* `in mode` {*C,F*}.	6
	`Reaction((`*EV*,{*D,LV*}`),`*PCtrl*`)` `within` $[220, 225]$ *ms* `in mode` *C* `post` 200 *ms*.	7
	`Reaction((`*EV*,{*D,LV*}`),`*PCtrl*`)` `within` $[170, 175]$ *ms* `in mode` *F*.	8
	PCtrl `occurs every` 5 *ms* `in mode` {*C,F*}.	9

Idle the system is activated (lines 3–4). A transition from *Idle* to *Evade* is automatically taken in safety-critical situations, i.e., without the need for manual activation (line 5). Depending on the active mode, the system shows different timing behavior. This is partly to save resources and partly to avoid unnecessary restrictions in the specifications. In *Cruise* mode, the system reacts to its inputs within 245 to 250 ms (line 6). In modes *Follow* and *Evade*, the reaction requires a shorter period of time (lines 7–9). Depending on the traffic situation, the *ACCwCA* switches between *Cruise*, *Follow*, and *Evade* until it is deactivated by a driver request (lines 10–11). To ensure continuous control, *Ctrl* and *Switch* are provided every 3 to 7 ms in all operating modes other than *Idle* (line 12).

The *ACCwCA* consists of three components, namely *ACC*, *Collision Avoidance*, and *Switching Logic*. Based on the definitions from Sect. 4, the top-level modes are mapped to combinations of the composed lower-level modes $M_{acc} \times M_{ca} \times M_{sl}$ by using a mode mapping function $\mu_{ACCwCA} : M_{acc} \times M_{ca} \times M_{sl} \rightarrow M_{ACCwCA}$. As a result of the combinatorics, mode combinations that lead to inconsistencies between the different specifications may arise, especially in transition phases. However, since these combinations are transient, a careful definition of suitable pre-phase and post-phase durations D_{pre} and D_{post} effectively prevents inconsistent behavior. The effects are explained below.

Table 3. Specification $\mathscr{C}_{ca}$ of the *Collision Avoidance* Component

A	{*D*,*LV*} occurs every 40 *ms* with jitter 5 *ms*.	1
	EV occurs every 10 *ms* with jitter 2 *ms*.	2
G	Reaction((*EV*,{*D*,*LV*}),set(*Mode*)) within (0, 1] *ms* {*E*,*N*}.	3
	Reaction(change(*Mode*,*E*),*Status.1*) within (0, 1] *ms* in mode *N*.	4
	Reaction((*EV*,{*D*,*LV*}),*Decel*) within [170, 175] *ms* in mode *E* post 0 *ms*.	5
	Reaction(change(*Mode*,*N*),*Status.0*) within (0, 1] *ms* in mode *E*.	6
	Decel occurs every 5 *ms* in mode *E* post 5 *ms*.	7

Table 4. Specification $\mathscr{C}_{sl}$ of the *Switching Logic* Component

A	*PCtrl* occurs every (0, ∞) *ms*.	1
	Status occurs every (0, ∞) *ms*.	2
	Decel occurs every 5 *ms* in mode *E* pre 5 *ms*.	3
G	Reaction(*PCtrl*,{*Ctrl*,*Switch*}) within 25 *ms* in mode *N*.	4
	Reaction(*Status.1*,set(*Mode*,*E*)) within (0, 1] *ms* in mode *N*.	5
	Reaction(*Decel*,{*Ctrl*,*Switch.2*}) within 25 *ms* in mode *E*.	6
	Reaction(*Status.0*,set(*Mode*,*N*)) within (0, 1] *ms* in mode *E*.	7

Adaptive Cruise Control. The *Adaptive Cruise Control* (ACC) component calculates control values in terms of *PCtrl* events. Its specification is shown in Table 2. The component has *Idle* (I), *Cruise* (C), and *Follow* (F) modes and is activated and deactivated by *Req* events (line 4–5). Situation-dependent changes between *Cruise* and *Follow* are possible at any time (line 6). In *Cruise* mode, the component takes 220 to 225 ms to react to inputs, whereby it has to react faster in *Follow* mode to respond timely to the behavior of the vehicle ahead (lines 7–8). *PCtrl* events are provided every 5 ms in both modes (line 9).

Collision Avoidance. The *Collision Avoidance* (*CA*) component, whose specification is given in Table 3, checks whether an emergency braking is required. It possesses *Normal* (N) and *Evade* (E) modes. As long as there is no hazardous situation, the *CA* is in *Normal* mode. If a violation of the critical distance is detected, it switches to *Evade* (line 3) and transmits a *Status* event with value 1 to inform the *Switching Logic* (line 4). The *CA* requires 170 to 175 ms to react to inputs (line 5). If the braking maneuver is completed, it switches back to *Normal* mode and outputs a *Status* event with a value of 0 (line 6). To prevent the system from running into inconsistent states, additional *Decel* events are output for 5 ms after leaving the *Evade* mode (line 7).

Switching Logic. The specification of the *Switching Logic* (*SL*) is presented in Table 4. The component has *Normal* (N) and *Evade* (E) modes. It receives *PCtrl*, *Decel*, and *Status* events as inputs (lines 1–3). Based on these values, it switches between *Normal* and *Evade* modes. In *Normal* mode, it forwards the

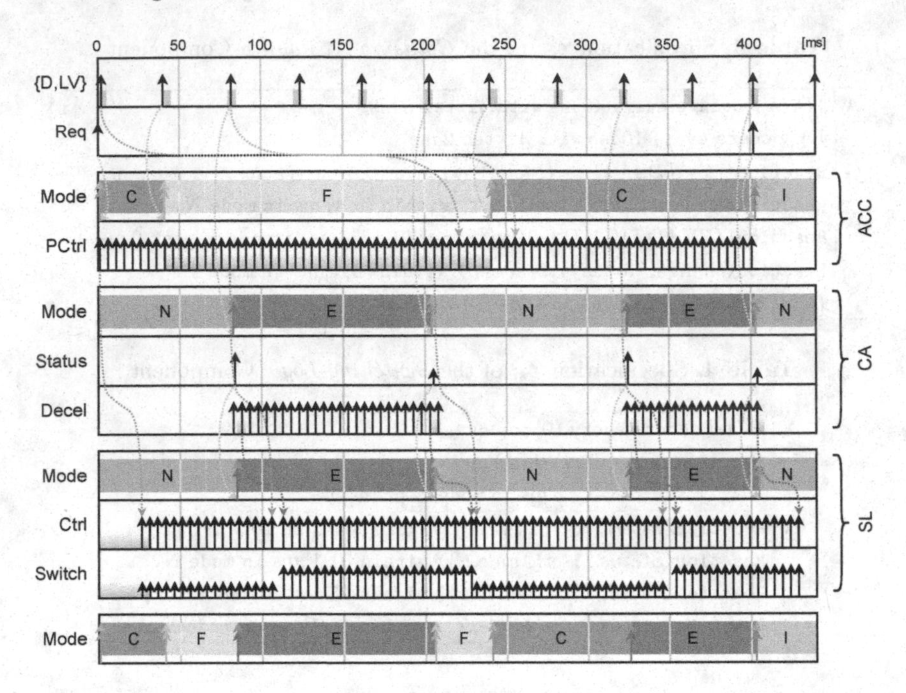

Fig. 5. Example Traces of the *ACC with Collision Avoidance*

received *PCtrl* and provides corresponding *Switch* events to enable a correct interpretation of the values (line 4). A mode change to *Evade* is triggered by receiving a *Status* event with value 1 (line 5). In *Evade* mode, it passes the *Decel* values with a *Switch* value of 2 (line 6). The occurrence of a *Status* event with a value of 0 triggers a transition to *Normal* mode (line 7).

Figure 5 depicts example traces that illustrate a possible system behavior. Here, we focus on the evolution of component modes as well as the propagation of mode changes through the overall system. Active pre- and post-phases are highlighted in green and orange color. The system is activated at $t = 0\,\text{ms}$ and deactivated again at $t = 400\,\text{ms}$. The top-level mode, which is presented in the bottom line, directly results from the composed lower-level modes. Note that *Cruise* and *Follow* modes are preempted by the high-priority *Evade* mode. In addition, the need for defining suitable pre- and post-phases is demonstrated. In the top-level specification, for example, a pre-phase is required to account for delays in providing initial results (see Table 1, line 12). Moreover, post-phases in $\mathscr{C}_{acc}$ ensure that the control values calculated in *Follow* mode are not overwritten by outdated values from the previous *Cruise* mode (see Table 2, line 5).

7 Conclusion

The presented approach enables a consistent handling of operating modes, mode transitions, and mode-dependent behavior in contract-based design. In contrast to related work, we performed the extensions on pattern level, which enables the use of infinite timed traces to characterize system behavior and facilitates seamless integration into an existing framework. The concepts allow a comprehensive consideration of timing aspects of mode-based systems and help to reduce verification complexity. In the future, we aim to investigate additional specification patterns and provide tool support for automated analyses.

References

1. Bebawy, Y., et al.: Incremental contract-based verification of software updates for safety-critical cyber-physical systems. In: International Conference on Computational Science and Computational Intelligence. IEEE (2020). https://doi.org/10.1109/CSCI51800.2020.00318
2. Benveniste, A., et al.: Contracts for system design. Found. Trends Electron. Des. Autom. **12**(2–3), 124–400 (2018). https://doi.org/10.1561/1000000053
3. Böde, E., et al.: Design paradigms for multi-layer time coherency in ADAS and automated driving (MULTIC). In: FAT Series. No. 302, Research Association for Automotive Technology (2017). https://www.vda.de/vda/de/aktuelles/publikationen/publication/fat-schriftenreihe-302
4. Böde, E., et al.: MULTIC-Tooling. In: FAT Series. No. 316, Research Association for Automotive Technology (2019). https://www.vda.de/vda/de/aktuelles/publikationen/publication/fat-schriftenreihe-316
5. Champion, A., Gurfinkel, A., Kahsai, T., Tinelli, C.: CoCoSpec: a mode-aware contract language for reactive systems. In: De Nicola, R., Kühn, E. (eds.) SEFM 2016. LNCS, vol. 9763, pp. 347–366. Springer, Cham (2016). https://doi.org/10.1007/978-3-319-41591-8_24
6. Damm, W., Dierks, H., Oehlerking, J., Pnueli, A.: Towards component based design of hybrid systems: safety and stability. In: Manna, Z., Peled, D.A. (eds.) Time for Verification. LNCS, vol. 6200, pp. 96–143. Springer, Heidelberg (2010). https://doi.org/10.1007/978-3-642-13754-9_6
7. Firus, V., Becker, S., Happe, J.: Parametric performance contracts for QML-specified software components. Electron. Not. Theoret. Comput. Sci. **141**(3), 73–90 (2005). https://doi.org/10.1016/j.entcs.2005.04.036
8. Kim, E.S., Arcak, M., Seshia, S.A.: A small gain theorem for parametric assume-guarantee contracts. In: Proceedings of the 20th International Conference on Hybrid Systems: Computation and Control, pp. 207–216. ACM (2017). https://doi.org/10.1145/3049797.3049805
9. Kugele, S., Marmsoler, D., Mata, N., Werther, K.: Verification of component architectures using mode-based contracts. In: ACM/IEEE International Conference on Formal Methods and Models for System Design, pp. 133–142. IEEE (2016). https://doi.org/10.1109/MEMCOD.2016.7797758
10. Reussner, R.H., Becker, S., Firus, V.: Component composition with parametric contracts. In: Tagungsband der Net. ObjectDays, pp. 155–169 (2004). https://sdqweb.ipd.kit.edu/publications/pdfs/reussner2004f.pdf

11. Reussner, R.H., Happe, J., Habel, A.: Modelling parametric contracts and the state space of composite components by graph grammars. In: Cerioli, M. (ed.) FASE 2005. LNCS, vol. 3442, pp. 80–95. Springer, Heidelberg (2005). https://doi.org/10.1007/978-3-540-31984-9_7
12. Sljivo, I., Gallina, B., Carlson, J., Hansson, H.: Strong and weak contract formalism for third-party component reuse. In: IEEE International Symposium on Software Reliability Engineering Workshops, pp. 359–364. IEEE (2013). https://doi.org/10.1109/ISSREW.2013.6688921

Coalition Formation with Multiple Alternatives of Interdependent Tasks

Youcef Sklab[1(✉)], Samir Aknine[2], Onn Shehory[3], and Hanane Ariouat[4]

[1] IRD, Sorbonne Université, UMMISCO, 93143 Bondy, France
youcef.sklab@ird.fr
[2] LIRIS Laboratory, Université Claude Bernard Lyon 1, Lyon, France
[3] Bar Ilan University, Ramat Gan, Israel
[4] IDHN, CY Cergy Paris University, Cergy, France

Abstract. In this paper, we consider the problem of coalition formation in multi-agent systems that exhibit externalities. We consider multiple self-interested agents each of which has a goal it needs to achieve. Each agent may have several alternative sets of dependent tasks leading it to achieve its goal. Execution of tasks may be more beneficial when done by a group of agents and not by a single agent. In fact, to achieve their goals, the agents need to form sequential interdependent coalitions to perform their tasks within an alternative. However, tasks dependencies lead to coalitions dependencies. To account for the effects of each coalition on the rest of the possible coalitions, the agents need to form all needed coalitions at once. This problem, denoted here as a *One-shot Coalition Formation Problem* ($\mathcal{OCFP}$), is quite challenging and particularly important for multi-agent system. We describe it and present a multi-lateral negotiation mechanism that solves it by allowing the agents to conduct iterative negotiations on their respective tasks within their alternatives. A heuristic-based approach that considers the distance between each agent's desired alternative and other agents' proposed coalitions is introduced and evaluated.

Keywords: Coalition formation · Multi-agent negotiation

1 Introduction

In this paper we introduce a new problem of coalition formation with externalities, called: *One-shot Coalition Formation Problem* ($\mathcal{OCFP}$), for which the coalition formation process should be considered as a one-shot activity. Coalition formation is defined as the process of forming a group of agents to perform a set of common tasks that the agents are unable to perform alone, or they do so inefficiently [11]. We consider a set of self-interested agents, each of which has several alternative sets of tasks, leading it to achieving its goal. We address cases in which task dependencies exist, hence each task may require outputs of other tasks for its performance. For example, Fig. 1 illustrates 4 agents $\{a_1, a_2, a_3, a_4\}$, representing 4 individuals, each wants to move from a starting city (nodes $\{a, b, c\}$) to a destination city (nodes $\{j, k\}$) and share its path segments costs (tasks $\{t_j \mid j = 1..15\}$) in order to reduce its total path cost. Each one may have several

A. Nouri et al. (Eds.): VECoS 2021, LNCS 13187, pp. 75–90, 2022.
https://doi.org/10.1007/978-3-030-98850-0_6

possible sequential tasks (paths) leading it to a goal (destination). Agent's sequential tasks are represented by a directed acyclic graph. In such a context, each agent may need to form a series of coalitions at different points in time to reach its goal. In the literature, this is performed as a sequential coalitions formation process (coalition after coalition). Doing so, can lead to the formation of coalitions with inferior utility and to sub-optimal task execution and goal satisfaction[1]. The problem here is that, after a coalition is formed at time t, another more beneficial coalition might no longer be possible at time $t+1$ because of conflicting dependencies among remaining tasks. The challenging question is how to avoid live-locks when getting commitments? In particular, due to task dependencies, each agent may prefer to get a commitment from others, before committing to any coalition. In fact, dependencies among tasks lead necessarily to dependencies among possible coalitions.

For example, consider the case of agent a_1, whose goal is to move from city ***a*** to city ***j*** (*cf.* Fig. 1). a_1 aims to locate which path minimizes its cost (we assume that if two agents perform a task together, they share the induced cost). Thus, it may prefer to form a coalition with a_2 for tasks t_1 and t_3, and then another coalition with a_3 and a_4 for t_5. a_1 may alternatively go through t_2. In fact, a_1 has to get the needed commitments from a_2, a_3 and a_4 at the same time. However, a_2 and a_4 also have several alternatives that they may consider before committing to any coalition. The main motivation of each agent is to reach its goal and minimize costs. Its focus is therefore not on a coalition for the current task but on a coalition structure that meets its final goal. A coalition structure comprises several coalitions in which the agent is involved. Each coalition is associated with a time interval in which its tasks are executed. We assume that, within each structure, the time intervals do not intersect and there are no temporal conflicts. We require that coalitions that form allow agents to reach their goals and minimize their costs. For this, the agents should take into account the dependencies between tasks, to avoid non-beneficial coalition structures. Note that, when following a task-by-task coalition formation approach[2] some tasks may become impossible to perform and some agents may become unavailable, negatively affecting benefits. Thus, the quality of a coalition depends both on endogenous and exogenous factors.

Plenty of coalition formation approaches have been proposed, but only a few of them deal with task dependencies [1,9,11]. Moreover, none of them facilitate the formation of multiple coalitions in a one-shot activity[3], as required in $\mathcal{OCFP}$.

Against this background, we introduce the *One-shot Coalition Formation Algorithm ($\mathcal{OCFA}$)*—a distributed coalition formation algorithm that solves $\mathcal{OCFP}$ and meets its unique requirements. Here, in forming coalition structures, each agent has to take into account inter-coalition dependencies, allowing it to reach its goal at a

[1] In this example, a path segment between two points represents a task. An example application scenario could be carpooling, where individuals want to reduce their travel costs between cities. In such cases, each agent may seek agreement of other agents to collaborative travel of its possible path segments before it agrees to such collaboration. This may cause conflicting situations and deadlocks.

[2] In a task-by-task approach, agents start by forming a coalition for the current task; then, they proceed and form a coalition for the next task, and so on.

[3] In the sens that the agents agree about all the coalitions to form before performing them.

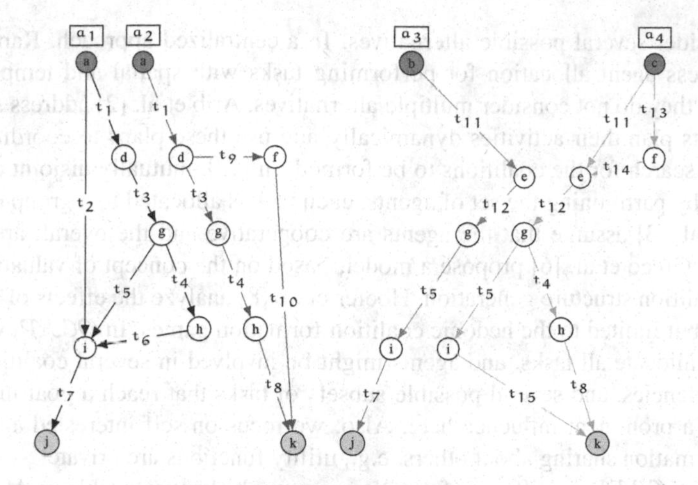

Fig. 1. Alternatives sets of agents a_1, a_2, a_3, a_4.

minimum cost (or maximum gain). The formation of one coalition may affect the gain expected from other possible coalitions. Note that $\mathcal{OCFP}$ is different from the problem of coalition structures generation (CSG), where the aim is to find the coalition structure that maximizes the social welfare, or minimizes the agents' deviation from their initial desired coalitions. Commonly, the CSG problem deals with partitioning the agents into mutually disjoint groups, to improve their performance [10]. In $\mathcal{OCFP}$, coalition structure generation focuses on identifying, for each agent, a profitable group of tasks from among multiple alternatives it has. It additionally seeks groups of agents—not necessarily disjoint—to perform the selected group of tasks. Moreover, in difference from the classical CSG problem, it considers the timing of sequentially executed dependent tasks. CSG may consider the time required for executing a task, but it does not deal with sequential task execution and the resulting temporal dependencies.

Our approach is heuristic-based, where the agents compute different metrics for making the decision on offers to be made, to be accepted or to be confirmed. Our mechanism comprises several steps: (i) Agents search for possible coalition structures, accounting for their utility functions and for dependencies among tasks. (ii) Agents' aspirations are derived, and taken into account in future proposals. (iii) At each round, agents estimate the gap between their proposals and those of the other agents. (iv) Agents rank their possible coalition structures using a ranking strategy based on a set of characteristic and valuation parameters.

The remainder of this paper is organized as follows. Section 2 discusses related work. Section 3 presents the one-shot coalition formation method. Section 4 presents the experimental evaluation and Sect. 5 concludes this paper.

2 Related Work

There are few studies on coalition formation that deal with dependencies among tasks. Shehory et al. [11] aim at allocating tasks to agents in a distributed approach, but they do not consider several possible alternatives. In a centralized approach, Ramchurn et al. [1] address agent allocation for performing tasks with spatial and temporal constraints, but they do not consider multiple alternatives. Arib et al. [2] address situations where agents plan their activities dynamically and use these plans to coordinate their actions and search for the coalitions to be formed. In [10], mutually disjoint coalitions are formed by partitioning the set of agents, each task is allocated to a group of agents. Bistaffa et al. [3] assume that the agents are cooperative and the overall approach is centralized. Greco et al. [6] propose a model, based on the concept of valuation structure, for coalition structure generation. Hoefer et al. [8] analyze the effects of structural constraints but limited to the hedonic coalition formation games. In $\mathcal{OCFP}$, we do not necessarily allocate all tasks, and agents might be involved in several coalitions. Task inter-dependencies, and several possible subsets of tasks that reach a goal in different ways, have a prominent influence here. Also, we focus on self-interested agents with partial information sharing about others, e.g., utility functions are private.

Note that $\mathcal{OCFP}$ is different from the commonly known problem: *Multi-Agent Planning* (MAP) [4,5,7,12] even if both assume agents with an individual set of tasks as input and as output a non-conflicting execution of their tasks. The major differences between MAP and $\mathcal{OCFP}$ are: (i) *coordination*: interdependent tasks are assigned to different agents, aiming at finding a non-conflicting execution of their plans. In $\mathcal{OCFP}$, the agents' alternatives are assumed to be non-conflicting if they are executed individually. So, the aim is not to coordinate task execution, but to identify which possible executions can be more beneficial. (ii) *joint tasks*: joint tasks are predefined and known by all agents. The aim is to coordinate agents' plan execution accordingly. In $\mathcal{OCFP}$, we assume that the tasks can be considered joint or disjoint depending on whether they are shared across alternatives or not. (iii) *negotiation*: negotiation is, mostly, about needed resources to perform tasks. In $\mathcal{OCFP}$, negotiation is about groups of tasks and agents to perform them. Furthermore, in planning via negotiation, it is assumed that the agents negotiate over the same set of tasks, which is different in $\mathcal{OCFP}$.

3 Coalition Formation Method

An $\mathcal{OCFP}$ is a tuple $\langle \mathcal{A}, \mathcal{T}, \mathcal{U}, \mathcal{G}, t_{limit} \rangle$ where $\mathcal{A} = \{a_1, a_2, ..., a_n\}$ is a set of self-interested agents, $\mathcal{T} = \{t_1, t_2, ..., t_m\}$ is a set of inter-dependent tasks, $\mathcal{U} = \{u_1, u_2, ..., u_n\}$ is a set of utility functions[4], one for each agent, $\mathcal{G} = \{g_1, g_2, ..., g_n\}$ is a set of goals, one for each agent, and $t_{limit} \in \mathbb{R}^+$ is the time limit for the coalition formation process. The aim of each agent a is to find a set of coalitions with respect to the dependencies to reach its goal g with the best possible value of u. A goal g can be reached by performing a set of tasks, that we call an ***alternative*** and denote α. An agent may have several possible alternatives leading it to its goal. For instance, agent a_1 (*cf.* Fig. 1) has 3 alternatives, a_2 has 2, a_3 has 1 and a_4 has 4 alternatives. We denote by Π_i the set of alternatives of an agent a_i.

In $\mathcal{OCFA}$ (Algorithm 1), we allow agents to identify beneficial coalitions to form, and to maintain an overall view on their possible coalitions during the coalition formation process. Specifically, we allow agents to engage in several negotiation threads with

[4] u is a function assessing an agent's benefit from a coalition.

different disjoint agent groups, for different task sets. We have devised a mechanism that consists of a protocol and a set of strategies. We decompose the coalition formation process into several distinctive steps: 1) *Exchange of alternatives*: The agents exchange their alternatives; 2) *Proposals generation*: The agents compute their coalitions proposals, and compute the coalition structures; 3) *Proposals*: The agents select a desired alternative, then exchange their proposals accordingly; 4) *Acceptances*: The agents exchange their acceptances about the exchanged proposals; 5) *Confirmations*: The agents exchange their confirmations about the accepted proposals. The $\mathcal{OCFA}$ begins with the computation alternatives, where each agent computes it own. Then, it sets the nextStep variable to the *Exchange of alternatives* step. As long as no coalitions are formed and the time limit is not reached, it loops and iterates through the steps: *Proposals generation*, *Proposals*, *Acceptances* and *Confirmations*.

Algorithm 1. $\mathcal{OCFA}()$

Require: : t_{limit};
1: $t_{current} \leftarrow 0$;
2: $t_{start} \leftarrow$ current time;
3: nextStep ← Exchange alternatives step;
4: endOfNegotiation ← false;
5: **while** (($t_{current} < t_{limit}$) **and** (**not** endOfNegotiation)) **do**
6: endOfNegotiation ← runStep(nextStep);
7: nextStep ← select the next step to run;
8: $t_{current} \leftarrow$ current time $- t_{start}$;
9: **end while**

The *Exchange of alternatives* step is followed by the *Proposals generation* step, during which each agent proceeds to analyzing each alternative's tasks and their corresponding dependencies in order to identify common tasks among them. A ***common task*** is common across two or more agents' alternatives. The set of *common tasks* of an agent a is denoted $ft_a = \{t \mid t \in \bigcup \alpha_a, \exists a' \in \mathcal{A} : a' \neq a \wedge t \in \bigcup \alpha_{a'}\}$. For instance, for agent a_1 (*cf.* Fig. 1), all its tasks are *common tasks* except $\{t_2, t_6\}$. That is, $ft_{a_1} = \{t_1, t_3, t_4, t_5, t_7\}$. Then, the common tasks are grouped into sets according to the agents' alternatives, that we call *common sets* of tasks (fs). Hence, for an agent a, the set of ***common sets*** is $\{fs_a = \langle \mathcal{A}_{fs_a}, \mathcal{T}_{fs_a} \rangle \mid \forall t \in \mathcal{T}_{fs_a}, \forall a' \in \mathcal{A}_{fs_a} : a \neq a' \Rightarrow t \in ft_a \cap ft_{a'}\}$. A tuple $\langle \mathcal{A}_{fs}, \mathcal{T}_{fs} \rangle$ is a combination of a set of successive common tasks $\mathcal{T}_{fs}$, with respect to the dependencies, which can be performed by a group of agents $\mathcal{A}_{fs}$. For instance, an example of common sets for agent a_1 is: $\{\langle \{a_1, a_2\}, \{t_1, t_3, t_4\} \rangle, \langle \{a_1, a_2\}, \{t_1, t_3\} \rangle, \langle \{a_1, a_3, a_4\}, \{t_5\} \rangle\}$. The set of ***common sets*** is then used to compute possible coalitions and coalition structures. We define a **coalition** as a tuple $c = \langle \mathcal{A}_c, \mathcal{T}_c \rangle$, where $\mathcal{A}_c \subseteq \mathcal{A}$ is a set of agents, $\mathcal{T}_c \subseteq \mathcal{T}$ a set of tasks and $\exists fs_a, fs_{a'}, a \neq a' : \mathcal{A}_c = \mathcal{A}_{fs_a} = \mathcal{A}_{fs_{a'}} \wedge \mathcal{T}_c = \mathcal{T}_{fs_a} = \mathcal{T}_{fs_{a'}}$. We assume that $|\mathcal{A}_c| \geq 2$, $|\mathcal{T}_c| \geq 1$ and agents in $\mathcal{A}_c$ have agreed to perform the tasks in $\mathcal{T}_c$. A **coalition structure** $cs = \{c \mid \exists \alpha : \mathcal{T}_c \subseteq \alpha\}$ is defined as a set of coalitions to perform tasks over an alternative α. We denote the set of all the coalitions of an agent a_i by $\mathcal{C}_i$ and its coalition structures by $\mathcal{CS}_i$. Once the coalition proposals are computed, they are grouped into coalition structures according to the agents' alternatives. This allows the agents to explore and keep updated their overall view on their alternatives. Hence, each alternative α corresponds to a coalition structures cs. We denote this association by $\mathcal{CS}(cs) = \alpha$. The set of the agents in a coalition structure is denoted $\Lambda(cs)$ and the set of its tasks is denoted $\Gamma(cs)$. Let's consider $\alpha_{1,3} = \{t_1, t_3, t_4, t_6, t_7\}$ (*cf.* Fig. 1), the third alternative of the agent a_1; examples of possible coalitions are: $c_1 = \langle\{a_1, a_2\}, \{t_1, t_3\}\rangle$, $c_2 = \langle\{a_1, a_2, a_4\}, \{t_4\}\rangle$, $c_3 = \langle\{a_1, a_3, a_4\}, \{t_5\}\rangle$, $c_4 = \langle\{a_1, a_3\}, \{t_7\}\rangle$, $c_5 = \langle\{a_1, a_2\}, \{t_1, t_3, t_4\}\rangle$. An example of a coalition structure that corresponds to $\alpha_{1,3}$ is: $cs_{1,3} = \{c_1, c_2, c_4\}$. So, for an alternative, it is not required that its associated coalition structure fulfills all of its tasks.

3.1 Multilateral Negotiation Protocol

The negotiation protocol $\mathcal{NP}$ comprises three main steps: it starts with the *Proposals* step, proceeds with the *Acceptances* step, and ends with the *Confirmations* step. The agents can evaluate their possible coalition structures at the end of each step. They exchange proposals, but this does not entail a commitment to any specific coalition structure. For instance, after sending proposals to different agent groups, the sender agent is not required send them acceptances even if it receives acceptances from most of the agents (but not from all[5]). As each coalition might affect other possible coalitions, a coalition proposal that has not been accepted by an agent might render all other coalition proposals impossible to achieve because of the dependencies. During the negotiation, the agents send and receive proposals, acceptances and confirmations for coalitions to be formed. If sent proposals have been followed by acceptances, agents can go ahead by confirmations or change their proposals and not accept those they have sent. They can also avoid confirming proposals they proposed and accepted earlier. In our protocol, an agent's confirmation of a proposal is not a binding agreement. Only mutually received confirmations about a specific coalition is a binding agreement. Therefore, once an agent has confirmed a proposal, it stays committed to it, unless none of the involved agents has sent a confirmation during the same negotiation round r.

Agents communicate via messages $m = (t, a, a', c)$ where t is the performative, $a \in \mathcal{A}$ is the sender, $a' \subseteq \mathcal{A}_c$ ($|\mathcal{A}_c| \geq 1$) is the receiver and c is a coalition proposal. The set of all the sent and received messages is denoted $\mathcal{M}$. To facilitate negotiation, we introduce some interaction rules $\mathbf{R}_i$:

$\mathbf{R}_1$: $m = (\texttt{Proposal}, a, a' \in \mathcal{A}_c, c)$ can be submitted about c several times, but not during the same negotiation round r.
$\mathbf{R}_2$: $m = (\texttt{Accept}, a, a' \in \mathcal{A}_{c'}, c')$ can be submitted, in a round r, only for agents a' that have sent proposals about c' to the agent a.
$\mathbf{R}_3$: $m = (\texttt{Confirm}, a, a' \in \mathcal{A}_{c'}, c')$ can be submitted, in a round r, only for agents a' that have accepted a proposal c'.
$\mathbf{R}_4$: During r, for two agents a and a', an agreement can be established about a coalition c, only if both agents have confirmed it.

[5] In case it receives acceptances from all of the agents that means the alternative it sought can be achieved, so the agent confirms its proposals.

To be involved in a negotiation process, an agent starts by selecting a coalition structure cs and sending its coalition proposals $c \in cs$ to the agents $a \in \mathcal{A}_c$ (**R**$_1$). Then it waits to receive other agents' proposals (during the same round r). If no proposals are received, the agent waits to the next round and selects another coalition structure cs' to propose[6]. Else, if there are received proposals, the agent can send back acceptances if the received proposals meet its expected utility regarding its sent proposals (**R**$_2$). Then, the agent waits for others' acceptances too. In case it receives acceptances that meet its expected utility, it replies to the senders with confirmations (**R**$_3$). Then, it waits for their confirmations. If it receives at least one confirmation, it must respect it, even if it does not fully meet its expected gain (**R**$_4$). If it receives no confirmation during the same round, it is considered free and returns to proposals step (**R**$_1$).

3.2 Ranking Coalition Structures

To engage in the negotiation protocol, an agent needs, at each *Proposals* step, to select a coalition structure cs from which it formulates its coalition proposals to other agents. To facilitate that, agents need to update their overall view on all possible coalition structures at each negotiation round. We introduce the *profile structure* ps, that should allow agents to characterize each of their coalition structures, and then, rank them accordingly.

Definition 1. *A* ***profile structure*** $ps = \langle t_1, t_2, ..., t_{|\bigcup(t \in \alpha \in \Pi)|} \rangle$ *of a set of alternatives* Π *is a vector that contains all the tasks in* Π.

That is, each agent's set of alternatives has a specific profile structure associated with it, which is defined according to the agent's set of tasks. For instance, the profile structure of the set of alternatives of agent a_1 (*cf.* Fig. 1) is: $ps_{a_1} = \langle t_2, t_7, t_1, t_3, t_5, t_4, t_6 \rangle$. We further define the *alternative profile*, which is a data representation structure characterizing each alternative of an agent.

Definition 2. *An* ***alternative profile*** $p^\alpha = \langle e_1, e_2, ..., e_{|ps|} \rangle$ *is a binary vector defined over an alternative* α *regarding a profile structure* ps*, where* $e_i \in \{0, 1\}$, $e_i = 1$ *means* $t_i \in \alpha$ *and* $e_i = 0$ *means* $t_i \notin \alpha$.

For instance, let's consider $\alpha_{1,3} = \{t_1, t_3, t_4, t_6, t_7\}$. Its profile is: $p^{\alpha_{1,3}} = \langle 0, 1, 1, 1, 0, 1, 1 \rangle$. Since a cs is associated with an α, for ease of presentation, for the rest of this paper we assume that $p^{cs} = p^\alpha$ (a coalition structure profile is the same profile of the alternative with which it is associated: $p^{\alpha_{1,3}} = p^{cs_{1,3}}$). Taking into account only the desired alternative of an agent for selecting the coalition structure to propose might lead to cyclic negotiation. To avoid this, an agent needs to consider other agents' proposals to derive their intentions. Hence, we introduce the agent's *coalition structure view*:

Definition 3. *A* ***coalition structure view*** $v_{cs}^{a'} = \{c' \mid \exists c \in cs : \mathcal{T}_c = \mathcal{T}_{c'} \wedge a \in \mathcal{A}_{c'}\}$ *is the set of received coalition proposals* c' *from an agent* a' *that are also proposed by* a *to* a' *as coalition proposals* c.

[6] Note that cs' might be the same as cs, depending on $\mathcal{P}$.

So, a coalition structure view $\upsilon_{cs}^{a'}$ is a coalition structure that contains only coalition proposals received from agent a' and that concerns only tasks in $\Gamma(cs)$. $\upsilon_{cs}^{a'}$ is called: a''s view on agent's a coalition structures cs. For instance, suppose that agent a_1 has received a set of coalition proposals from a_2 about the tasks $\{t_1, t_3, t_4\}$ at round $r = 2$. So, for a_1, the coalition structure view of a_2 on $cs_{1,3}$ is $\upsilon_{cs_{1,3}}^{a_2} = \{c'_1 = \langle\{a_1, a_2\}, \{t_1, t_3\}\rangle, c'_2 = \langle\{a_1, a_2, a_4\}, \{t_4\}\rangle\}$ and its profile is $p^{\upsilon_{cs_{1,3}}^{a_2}} = \langle 0, 0, 1, 1, 0, 1, 0\rangle$.

During the negotiations, the agents need to estimate how much an alternative α, represented by a coalition structure cs, is close to the proposals sent by other agents. For this purpose, we introduce the *footprint* function σ which computes how a coalition structure cs, represented by its profile p^{cs}, of agent a is close to another agent's a' view on cs, denoted by $\upsilon_{cs}^{a'}$ and represented by its profile $p^{\upsilon_{cs}^{a'}}$. σ's value is defined as:

$$\sigma(p^{cs}, p^{\upsilon_{cs}^{a'}}) = \sum_{e_i \in p^{cs}, e'_i \in p^{\upsilon_{cs}^{a'}}}^{i=0..|ps|} (e_i @ e'_i), \text{ where,}$$

$$e_i @ e'_i = \begin{cases} 1, \text{ if}: e_i = e'_i = 1 \\ 1/|ps|, \text{ if}: (e_i = 1 \wedge e'_i = 0) \vee (e_i = 0 \wedge e'_i = 1) \\ 0, \text{ if}: e_i = e'_i = 0 \end{cases}$$

The footprint of the coalition structure $cs_{1,3}$ regarding the proposals of a_2 is: $\sigma(p^{cs_{1,3}}, p^{\upsilon_{cs_{1,3}}^{a_2}}) = \langle 0, 1, 1, 1, 0, 1, 1\rangle @ \langle 0, 0, 1, 1, 0, 1, 0\rangle = (0@0) + (1@0) + (1@1) + (1@1) + (0@0) + (1@1) + (1@0) = 0 + 1/7 + 1 + 1 + 0 + 1 + 1/7 = 3.29$.

For an agent a, the *footprint* is computed for each round r between the coalition structure cs of the sent coalition proposals and other agents' views on cs. But this value alone is not sufficient to reflect the global view on possible coalition structures according to agents' proposals. Hence, we introduce the *distance* function π_{cs}^r to estimate the evolution made during negotiation regarding each alternative. It measures the distance between cs and all the coalition structure views on cs of other agents $a' \neq a$. Its value is computed at each round $r > 1$, regarding $(r - 1)$ as follows:

$$\pi_{cs}^r = \sum_{a' \in \Lambda(cs)} \sigma^r(p^{cs}, p^{\upsilon_{cs}^{a'}}) - \sigma^{r-1}(p^{cs}, p^{\upsilon_{cs}^{a'}})$$

This allows agents to estimate how and which alternative is becoming close (or not) to other agents' proposals. For instance, suppose that a_1 has received a set of coalition proposals $c = \{\langle\{a_2, a_1\}, \{t_1\}\rangle\}$ from a_2 at round $r = 3$ (a_1 wants to try alternative $\alpha_{1,3} = \{t_1, t_3, t_4, t_6, t_7\}$ and a_2 wants to try alternative $\alpha_{2,2} = \{t_1, t_9, t_{10}\}$). For a_1, $p^{\upsilon_{cs_{1,3}}^{a_2}} = \langle 0, 0, 1, 0, 0, 0, 0\rangle$. So, the footprint: $\sigma(p^{cs_{1,3}}, p^{\upsilon_{cs_{1,3}}^{a_2}}) = 1.57$. Then, for a_1, the distance of $cs_{1,3}$ according to the received coalition proposals from a_2 between $r = 2$ and $r = 3$ is: $\pi_{cs_{1,3}}^3(\sigma^3, \sigma^2) = \sigma^3 - \sigma^2 = \sigma^3(p^{cs_{1,3}}, p^{\upsilon_{cs_{1,3}}^{a_2}}) - \sigma^2(p^{cs_{1,3}}, p^{\upsilon_{cs_{1,3}}^{a_2}}) = 1.57 - 3.29 = -1.72$. The distance π_{cs}^r is interpreted by a, regarding a' as follows ($\mathcal{CS}(cs) = \alpha$):

- if $\pi_{cs}^r \geq 1$ Strong convergence: $\exists t \in \alpha$ which was not proposed by a' in $r - 1$ but proposed in r;

- if $0 < \pi^r_{cs} < 1$ Weak divergence: $\exists t \notin \alpha$ which was proposed by a' in $r-1$, but not proposed in r;
- if $0 > \pi^r_{cs} > -1$ Weak convergence: $\exists t \notin \alpha$ which was not proposed by a' in $r-1$, but proposed in r (having a new proposed task t even if $t \notin \alpha$ may render an alternative other than α close to the proposals of a');
- if $\pi^r_{cs} \leq -1$ Strong divergence: $\exists t \in \alpha$ which was proposed by a' in $r-1$ but not proposed in r;
- if $\pi^r_{cs} = 0$: no evolution.

In addition to the estimated distance, which is based on the presence and absence of tasks in agents' proposals and considers only two consecutive rounds (the current round r, and $r-1$), the agents need to take into account earlier information to reflect trends in the whole negotiation process and update the ranking order of their coalition structures. Hence, we introduce several parameters with concern to different aspects, as explained hereafter:

- ***Estimated utility weight*** (ε): is a normalized value ($\varepsilon \in [0, 1[$) of the coalition structure estimated utility $u(cs)$: $\varepsilon = \begin{cases} 1 - \frac{u(\delta)}{u(cs)}, & \text{if } u(\delta) \neq 0 \\ 0, & \text{otherwise} \end{cases}$ where $u(\delta)$ denotes the agent utility reference value[7] and $u(cs) > u(\delta)$. We assume that if $u(cs) \leq u(\delta)$, cs will not be considered for negotiation.
- ***Tasks weight*** (rf): is a value reflecting how much tasks $t \in \Gamma(cs)$ are desired by other agents through their coalition proposals: $rf = \frac{\sum_{c \in cs} \sum_{t \in \mathcal{T}_c} \frac{fr(t)}{|\mathcal{A}_c|}}{\sum_{t' \in \mathcal{T}} fr(t')}$ where $fr(t)$ returns the number of coalition proposals c' for which $t \in \mathcal{T}_{c'}$.
- ***Coalition structure weight*** (w): is a value estimating the importance of a coalition structure cs, regarding other coalition structures: $\omega = \frac{rec(cs)}{|\Lambda(cs)|}$ where $rec(cs)$ returns the number of agents that have sent coalition proposals $c' : \mathcal{T}_{c'} \cap \Gamma(cs) \neq \emptyset$. Note that, while rf focuses on the received proposals concerning a task t, w focuses on the agents that have sent proposals about tasks $t \in \Gamma(cs)$. The former returns a value according to the number of tasks in an alternative set, and the latter returns a value according to the number of agents involved in a coalition structure.
- ***Sent proposals weight*** (sf): is a value estimating the importance of a coalition structure cs for an agent, during the negotiation: $sf = \frac{sent(cs)}{r}$ where $sent(cs)$ returns the number of times cs was selected by the agent to send its coalition proposals, and r is the current negotiations round. The rationale here is that, the more a coalition structure cs is selected, the more it is preferred by the agent.
- ***Distance weight*** (ϑ): is a normalized value of the distance π^r_{cs}:

$$\vartheta = \begin{cases} -\frac{\pi^r_{cs} \times |\alpha|}{|\mathcal{T}|^2}, & \text{if } -1 < \pi^r_{cs} < 0 \text{ or } 0 < \pi^r_{cs} < 1 \\ \frac{\pi^r_{cs} \times |\alpha|}{|\mathcal{T}|^2}, & \text{otherwise} \end{cases}$$

where r indicates the current round of negotiation. $\mathcal{NP}$ allows agents to update their view about the possible coalition structures by keeping updated the above set of

[7] $u(\delta)$ can be the minimum utility an agent can get if it performs its preferred tasks alone.

parameters, that we call, *characteristic parameters* $\mathcal{P} = \{\varepsilon, \omega, rf, sf, \vartheta\}$, where $\forall e \in \mathcal{P} : -1 \leq e \leq 1$ prior to each proposals' step. Additionally, to allow agents to rank their coalition structures during negotiation, we propose a ranking function named *coalition structure acceptance indicator* $\mathcal{V}_{cs} : (\mathcal{P} \times \tilde{\mathcal{P}}) \longrightarrow \mathbb{R}$, which is based on $\mathcal{P}$ and a set of *valuation parameters* $\tilde{\mathcal{P}} = \{\tilde{\varepsilon}, \tilde{\omega}, \tilde{rf}, \tilde{sf}, \tilde{\vartheta}\}$, where $e \in \tilde{\mathcal{P}} : e > 0$. $\tilde{\mathcal{P}}$ is assumed to be initialized by the user to provide its preferences as follows:

- $\tilde{\varepsilon}$: valuation of the *Estimated utility weight* (ε).
- $\tilde{\omega}$: valuation of the *Coalition structure weight* (w).
- $\tilde{rf}$: valuation of the *Tasks weight* (rf).
- $\tilde{sf}$: valuation of the *Sent proposals weight* (sf).
- $\tilde{\vartheta}$: valuation of the *Distance weight* (ϑ).

The valuation parameters values are computed at each round using the heuristic in (Algorithm 2), according to π. These parameters reflect the negotiation trend, thus allowing agents to explore the set $\mathcal{CS}$ by establishing a ranking order over it. The value of $\mathcal{V}_{cs}$ is defined as follows:

$$\mathcal{V}_{cs}(\mathcal{P}, \tilde{\mathcal{P}}) = (\tilde{\varepsilon})^{\varepsilon} + (\tilde{\omega})^{\omega} + (\tilde{rf})^{rf} + (\tilde{\vartheta})^{\vartheta} - (\tilde{sf})^{sf}$$

At the beginning (round $r = 1$), each agent ranks its coalition structures by using its estimated utility, $u(cs)$, defined as the expected utility if all involved agents $a \in \Lambda(cs)$ accept or confirm to perform jointly all the tasks $t \in \Gamma(cs)$. For rounds $r > 1$, prior to each *Proposals* step, the agents use $\mathcal{V}_{cs}$ to rank their coalition structures. In addition to the characteristic parameters in $\mathcal{P}$, the valuation parameters in $\tilde{\mathcal{P}}$ are used as a means to introduce a valuation mechanism, allowing agents to prefer one parameter over others in $\mathcal{V}_{cs}$, according to the observed evolution in the negotiation. In doing so, agents will be able to dynamically react and select a coalition structure according to a specific characteristic parameter by increasing their valuation of that parameter.

In fact, having one valuation parameter notably superior to the others, makes the agent select the coalition structures, mostly, according to its associated characteristic parameter. For instance, if a user (represented by an agent) wants to find a coalition structure with a low cost, he can introduce a higher value of the valuation parameter $\tilde{\varepsilon}$. Note that such parameter preference may incure, in some cases, undesirable results. For example, having a higher value of $\tilde{\varepsilon}$ might lead agents to negotiate only the most beneficial coalition structures. In this case, a larger value of the valuation parameter $\tilde{sf}$ can force agents to alternate the proposals they send and explore more possibilities. For example, (in the heuristic in Algorithm 2), when $\pi = 0$ which means there is no evolution in the negotiation, we cancel the effect of the *Distance weight* and increase the valuation of the *sent proposals weight* (which will be subtracted in $\mathcal{V}_{cs}$) to decrease an agent's value of coalition structures that are sent more frequently. In doing so, we guarantee that the agent will adopt an exploration attitude and try to find a coalition structure by exploring different coalition structures. This aims to avoid cyclic negotiation where each agent proposes the most preferred proposals in cs again and again, even though cs cannot be a solution.

Algorithm 2. valuationHeuristic()

```
1: if (π ≥ 1) then
2:     ϑ̃ = ϑ̃ + ϑ̃ ∗ π;
3:     s̃f = s̃f ∗ (ϑ̃)^ϑ;
4: else
5:     if (π > 0 & π < 1) then
6:         s̃f = s̃f + (ϑ̃)^ϑ;
7:         ϑ̃ = (ϑ̃)^−ϑ;
8:     else
9:         if (π == 0) then
10:            if ϑ > 1 then
11:                ϑ = 1;
12:            end if
13:            s̃f+ = (ω̃)^ω + (ε̃)^ε
14:            s̃f = s̃f + (s̃f ∗ log(passedTime));
15:        else
16:            if (π < 0 & π > −1) then
17:                ϑ̃ = ϑ̃ + (ϑ̃ ∗ (−π));
18:            else
19:                if (π ≤ −1) then
20:                    s̃f = s̃f + (ϑ̃)^ϑ;
21:                    r̃f = r̃f + (ϑ̃)^ϑ;
22:                    ϑ̃ = 1;
23:                end if
24:            end if
25:        end if
26:    end if
27: end if
```

3.3 Decision Making

Agents' decisions are made based on their utility from the proposals, and acceptances at hand at each step. Ahead of the negotiation, an agent sets its referred utility value, denoted $u(\delta)$. After the first ranking (r = 1), an agent selects the coalition structure cs that has the highest $u(cs) > u(\delta)$ and sends all of the coalition proposals $c \in cs$ to all of the involved agents $a \in \mathcal{A}_c$. We assume that if $u(cs) = u(\delta)$, the agent will prefer to perform the tasks $t \in \Gamma(cs)$ alone. After sending all of the coalition proposals $c \in cs$, the agent updates its estimated utilities $u(cs)$ according to the received coalition proposals and decides whether to accept proposals (if $u(cs) > u(\delta)$), or not. In case that $u(cs) \leq u(\delta)$, it will select another coalition structure cs' to propose. After sending acceptances about cs, the agent updates its estimated utility based on the received acceptances. If $u(cs) > u(\delta)$, it sends confirmations to the agents that have sent it acceptances and, then, waits to receive their confirmations too.

4 Experimental Evaluation

In this section, we experimentally evaluate $\mathcal{OCFA}$, (implemented in Java). To this aim, we assume that each task has a public cost $O^+(t)$, known by all the agents and a private cost $O^-(t)$, specific for each agent and only known by the owner. That is, for each agent, the cost of each task is $O(t) = O^+(t) + O^-(t)$. The cost of a coalition structure cs is denoted $O(cs)$. We denote by O^{max} the $cs \in \mathcal{CS}$ maximum cost and O^{min} the

$cs \in \mathcal{CS}$ minimum cost. Additionally, we introduce an allowed cost[8] to assume by each agent during negotiations as: $O^* = \frac{O^{max}+O^{min}}{2}$. The estimated utility[9] of each coalition $u(c) = \sum_{t \in \mathcal{T}_c} O(t) - [\sum_{t \in \mathcal{T}_c}(\frac{O^+(t)}{|\mathcal{A}_c|}) + O^-(t)]$, and $u(cs) = \sum_{c \in cs} u(c)$. So, the agents will search for a coalition structure where its cost $O(cs) < O^*$ and its utility verifies $u(cs) > u(\delta)$. We assume that the reference utility $u(\delta) = 0$.

In the first experiment, we consider 3 agents $\mathcal{A} = \{a_1, a_2, a_3\}$ with a limitation rate $(1 \geqslant O^\bullet \geqslant 0)$ on the allowed cost for each agent. We additionally redefine O^* as $O^* = O^* \times O^\bullet$. Further, for ease of presentation, we assume that all agents have the same alternatives set (same tasks) but with different costs. We assume that each alternatives set has 12 tasks, forming six alternatives $(\alpha_1, \alpha_2, \alpha_3, \alpha_4, \alpha_5, \alpha_6)$. First, the results (Fig. 2) show that, starting from $O^\bullet = 1$ to $O^\bullet = 0.52$, the more we decrease $O^\bullet$, the more the negotiation requires more rounds to reach a solution. In fact, lower values of $O^\bullet$ make the agents accept lower costs, so, seek for higher gains. For instance, for $O^\bullet = 0.60$ a solution was found at round $r = 11$ and for $O^\bullet = 0.52$ a solution was found at $r = 24$.

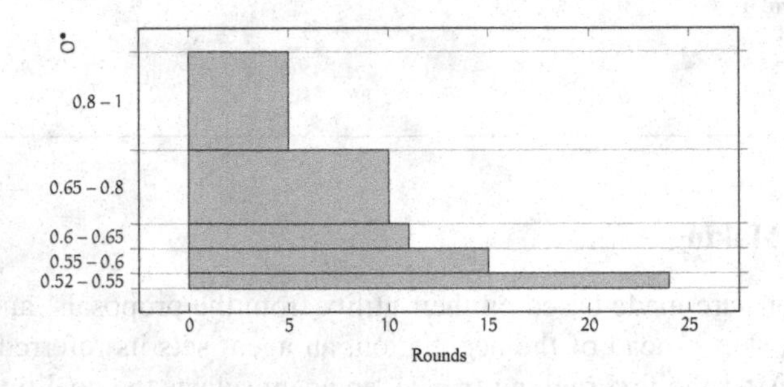

Fig. 2. Cost limit vs. negotiation rounds. Here, we studied the effect of decreasing O^* during negotiation on the number of rounds to find a solution. The experimental settings we consider are $\tilde{\mathcal{P}} = \{\tilde{\varepsilon} = 30, \tilde{\omega} = 2, \tilde{rf} = 5, \tilde{sf} = 7, \tilde{\vartheta} = 15\}$, $O^+(t) = 30$, $\forall t \in \mathcal{T}$, and O^- is randomly generated: $0 > O^-(t) < 20$ for each task.

Second, we study the way the value of $\mathcal{V}_{cs}$ is obtained. Hence, we focus on the values of the elements $\tilde{\varepsilon}^{\varepsilon}$, $\tilde{\omega}^{\omega}$, $\tilde{rf}^{rf}$, $\tilde{\vartheta}^{\vartheta}$ and $\tilde{sf}^{sf}$ that define the value of $\mathcal{V}_{cs}$. To this end, we initialize $\tilde{\mathcal{P}} = \{\tilde{\varepsilon} = 8, \tilde{\omega} = 2, \tilde{rf} = 20, \tilde{sf} = 15, \tilde{\vartheta} = 5\}$, fix $O^\bullet = 0.52$ and keep the same alternatives sets as in the first experiment. Here, we have considered two cases for the agent a_1, which has an initial order over its alternatives, from the most beneficial to the less beneficial: $\alpha_6, \alpha_3, \alpha_1, \alpha_2, \alpha_5, \alpha_4$. In the first case, we study the contribution rate (the percentage of $\tilde{\varepsilon}^{\varepsilon}$, $\tilde{\omega}^{\omega}$, $\tilde{rf}^{rf}$, $\tilde{\vartheta}^{\vartheta}$ and $\tilde{sf}^{sf}$ values in $\mathcal{V}_{cs}$ value) for

[8] The allowed cost defines a maximum value beyond which agents will not agree to spend more to achieve their goal. With a smaller value of the allowed cost, the agents try arrive at a lower cost coalition structure (if exists). This could therefore make it difficult to find agreements.

[9] Note that the choice of those formulas to compute the estimated utility is not motivated by a particular objective. In fact, the user can use his own formula to compute it, depending on the application use case.

the most beneficial alternative α_6 (*cf.* Fig. 3A) (which is the worst for other agents), and in the second case, we study the contribution rate for the final selected alternative α_3 which has led to the solution (*cf.* Fig. 3B). During the negotiation, a solution was found at round $r = 10$. The sent proposals from a_1 to the others at round at $r = 1$: were about α_6, at $r = 2 : \alpha_4$, at $r = 3 : \alpha_6$, at $r = 4 : \alpha_6$, at $r = 5 : \alpha_6$, at $r = 6 : \alpha_5$, at $r = 7 : \alpha_5$, at $r = 8 : \alpha_5$, at $r = 9 : \alpha_3$ and at $r = 10 : \alpha_3$. The results show that, in the first case (*cf.* Fig. 3A), for $r < 6$ where the most sent proposals were those for α_6, the value $\tilde{sf}^{sf}$ was more substantial in rounds where $\pi < 0$ ($r = 1, r = 3, r = 5$). After that, for $r \in [6, 8]$, $\tilde{sf}^{sf}$ was less substantial, as proposals other than α_6 were sent, induced by substantial values of $\tilde{\varepsilon}^{\varepsilon}$, $\tilde{\omega}^{\omega}$, $\tilde{rf}^{rf}$, $\tilde{\vartheta}^{\vartheta}$. For $r = 9$, the agent has observed an important convergence with the other agents, then the contribution of $\tilde{\vartheta}^{\vartheta}$ value in $\mathcal{V}_{cs}$ of α_3 has been adjusted to be the most substantial value in order to keep α_3 for the next round which has led to the solution at round $r = 10$.

In the second case (*cf.* Fig. 3B), as the alternative α_3 was in the second position in the first established order, the results show that during negotiation ($r \leq 8$) the most substantial value is that of the estimated cost $\tilde{\varepsilon}^{\varepsilon}$. The other values were mostly at the same level until round $r = 9$, during which the agent has observed an important convergence between others' proposals and the alternative α_3. Therefore, the value of $\tilde{\vartheta}^{\vartheta}$ was adjusted to maintain it for the next round, which has led to an effective solution at $r = 10$.

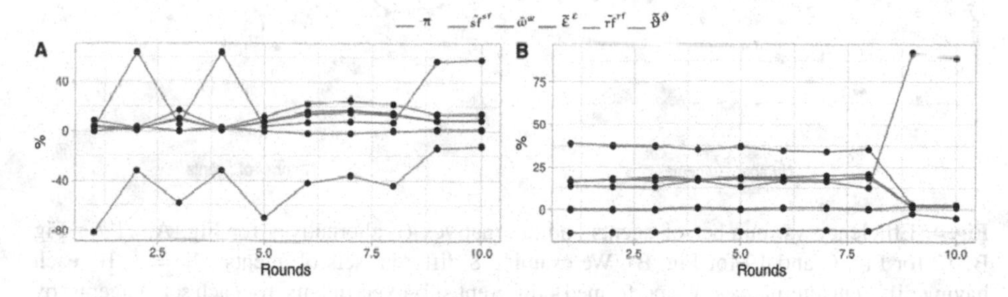

Fig. 3. The percentage (%) of $\tilde{\varepsilon}^{\varepsilon}$, $\tilde{\omega}^{\omega}$, $\tilde{rf}^{rf}$, $\tilde{\vartheta}^{\vartheta}$ and $\tilde{sf}^{sf}$ values in $\mathcal{V}_{cs}$ value at each round for $\mathcal{V}_{\alpha_6}$ (Fig. A) and $\mathcal{V}_{\alpha_3}$ (Fig. B).

In the third experiment, we aim at evaluating the $\mathcal{OCFA}$ by varying the number of negotiating agents and the number of alternatives in their respective alternatives sets. For this experiment, we introduce a new performance measure: *Efficiency* (φ), which is computed as an average of the gained profits across all agents over multiple experiments:

$$\varphi = \frac{\sum_1^n \left(\frac{\sum_{a_i \in \mathcal{A}} u_i(\alpha_{i,k})}{|\mathcal{A}|} \right)}{N_{exp}}$$

where n is the number of runs within an experiment given O_i^*, N_{exp} is the number of the experiments and the utility of the selected alternative $\alpha_{i,k}$ for an agent is: $u_i(\alpha_{i,k}) = \frac{O_i^- - O_i^f(\alpha_{i,k})}{O_i^-}$ where $O_i^f(\alpha_{i,k})$ is the effective cost of $\alpha_{i,k}$ according to the formed coalitions and, O_i^-, is the minimum individual cost (*i.e.* the best cost that an agent can get when performing the preferred tasks alone).

As there is no comparable approach with our algorithm in the literature, we compare our results to the *Best Alternative Algorithm* ($\mathcal{BAA}$). In fact, we didn't a comparison with an optimal solution approach, because the agents are selfish and do not reveal their private information. Hence, such a solution approach (for instance, by a linear programming solver) is not feasible in our problem. In $\mathcal{BAA}$, each agent orders all of its possible alternatives, it then selects its preferred alternative α_i^* and proposes the coalition structure cs (α^{cs}) associated with it to the involved agents $a \in \Lambda(sc)$. After that, each agent $a \in \Lambda(cs)$ that has received a proposal concerning a coalition $c \in cs$ it proposed, will accept and confirm it to its respective sender[10].

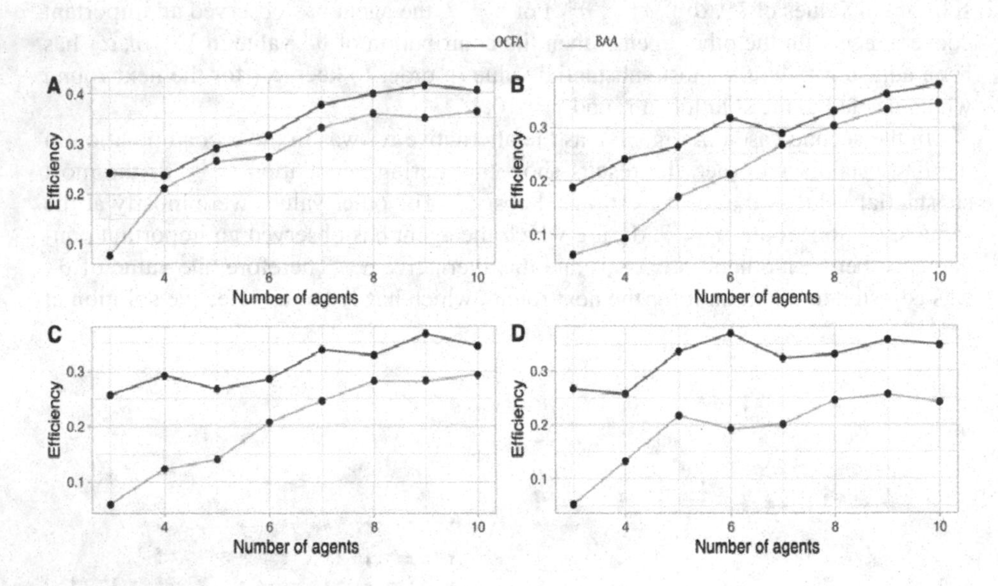

Fig. 4. Efficiency vs. number of agents and alternatives (6 alternatives for Fig. A, 11 for Fig B, 12 for Fig. C and 19 for Fig. B). We examine 8 different sets of agents $|\mathcal{A}| = 3..10$, each having different alternatives. We performed 4 different sub-experiments, for each set of agents, by varying the number of alternatives per agent (6, 11, 12, 19). We considered 10 values of $O^\bullet \in \{1, 0.95, 0.90, 0.85, 0.80, 0.75, 0.70, 0.65, 0.60, 0.55\}$. The results represent the average of 20 runs for each value of $O^\bullet$.

As can be observed in Figs. 4A, 4B, 4C and 4D, the efficiency of $\mathcal{OCFA}$ is clearly higher than the efficiency of $\mathcal{BAA}$. We remark that the efficiency is in correlation with both the number of agents and the number of alternatives. Note however that higher efficiency values were recorded for $\{6, 11\}$ alternatives and $|\mathcal{A}| \in \{8, 9, 10\}$ agents. The variation in efficiency values when increasing the number of agents is more significant in cases where the agents have less alternatives. The first observation is that, for

[10] Here, there is no negotiation among agents and each considers only its preferred alternative α_i^*, and agrees to jointly perform the tasks that are common to its preferred alternative and to the preferred coalition structures of the other agents.

both approaches, the interval between the minimum and the maximum efficiency values is inversely proportional to the number of alternatives. As we increase the number of alternatives, we get a smaller interval. The second observation is that, when we increase the number of alternatives in the $\mathcal{BAA}$ approach, the efficiency interval becomes smaller because of the maximum bound which becomes smaller (from 0.36 to 0.25), and the minimum bound remains mostly the same (around 0.05). In $\mathcal{OCFA}$ the efficiency interval becomes smaller because of the minimum bound which becomes higher (from around 0.21, 0.18 to 0.25), and the maximum bound remains mostly the same (around 0.36, 0.38). The third observation is that, while increasing the number of alternatives, the gap between the efficiency values of the two approaches becomes notably important; for 19 alternatives, the maximum value for $\mathcal{BAA}$ equals the minimum value for $\mathcal{OCFA}$ (*cf.* Fig. 4D).

5 Conclusion

In this paper, we addressed a new problem of coalition formation as a one-shot activity, where self-interested agents have several alternatives to reach different goals. Our approach is based on a multilateral negotiation protocol $\mathcal{NP}$, which is designed in a cyclic way over three main steps. During each one, agents compute a set of characteristic parameters $\mathcal{P}$ to use in a heuristic function in order to establish a ranking order over possible coalition structures. Our experimental evaluation shows that our approach allows the agents to converge to a solution. This is facilitated by an adjustable raking function that takes into account the trends of the negotiation. In this paper, we did not address scalability issues, and we deliberately did not consider strategic manipulation against our protocol. These aspects are out of scope of this paper. Furthermore, our experiments did not examine time constraints. Such constraints will be addressed in future work too.

References

1. Coalition formation with spatial and temporal constraints. In: AAMAS 2010, International Foundation for Autonomous Agents and Multiagent Systems, Richland, SC, May 2010
2. Arib, S., Aknine, S.: A plan based coalition formation model for multi-agent systems. In: 2011 IEEE/WIC/ACM International Conferences on Web Intelligence and Intelligent Agent Technology, vol. 2, pp. 365–368, August 2011
3. Bistaffa, F., Farinelli, A., Chalkiadakis, G., Ramchurn, S.D.: A cooperative game-theoretic approach to the social ridesharing problem. Artif. Intell. **246**, 86–117 (2017)
4. Buzing, P., Mors, A.T., Valk, J., Witteveen, C.: Coordinating self-interested planning agents. Auton. Agent. Multi-Agent Syst. **12**(2), 199–218 (2006)
5. Cox, J., Durfee, E.: Efficient and distributable methods for solving the multiagent plan coordination problem. Multiagent Grid Syst. Plan. Multiagent Syst. **5**(4), 373–408 (2009)
6. Greco, G., Guzzo, A.: Constrained coalition formation on valuation structures: formal framework, applications, and islands of tractability. Artif. Intell. **249**, 19–46 (2017)
7. Hadad, M., Kraus, S., Ben-Arroyo Hartman, I., Rosenfeld, A.: Group planning with time constraints. Ann. Math. Artif. Intell. **69**(3), 243–291 (2013). https://doi.org/10.1007/s10472-013-9363-9

8. Hoefer, M., Vaz, D., Wagner, L.: Dynamics in matching and coalition formation games with structural constraints. Artif. Intell. **262**, 222–247 (2018). https://doi.org/10.1016/j.artint.2018.06.004. https://www.sciencedirect.com/science/article/pii/S0004370218303151
9. Mahdiraji, H.A., Razghandi, E., Hatami-Marbini, A.: Overlapping coalition formation in game theory: a state-of-the-art review. Expert Syst. Appl. **174**, 114752 (2021). https://doi.org/10.1016/j.eswa.2021.114752. https://www.sciencedirect.com/science/article/pii/S0957417421001937
10. Rahwan, T., Michalak, T.P., Wooldridge, M., Jennings, N.R.: Coalition structure generation: a survey. Artif. Intell. **229**, 139–174 (2015)
11. Shehory, O., Kraus, S.: Methods for task allocation via agent coalition formation. Artif. Intell. **101**(1), 165–200 (1998)
12. Tonino, H., Bos, A., de Weerdt, M., Witteveen, C.: Plan coordination by revision in collective agent based systems. Artif. Intell. **142**(2), 121–145 (2002)

Author Index

Printed in the United States
by Baker & Taylor Publisher Services